SALUTE... HE MOVES!

First edition

Published in 2011 by
WOODFIELD PUBLISHING LTD
West Sussex ~ England ~ PO21 5EL
www.woodfieldpublishing.co.uk

ISBN 1-84683-095-8

The views and opinions expressed throughout
this book are those of the author alone and do
not reflect those of HMG, MOD, the RAF or any
government agency.

v3.2 2012

Salute...
He Moves!

*A personal reflection on four decades
with the Royal Air Force ~ 1952-90*

PETER HOLLAND

Woodfield

Woodfield Publishing Ltd

Woodfield House ~ Babsham Lane ~ Bognor Regis ~ West Sussex ~ PO21 5EL
telephone 01243 821234 ~ **e-mail** enquiries@woodfieldpublishing.co.uk

Interesting and informative books on a variety of subjects

For full details of all our published titles, visit our website at
www.woodfieldpublishing.co.uk

I dedicate this book to Kerstin and our children, Peter, David and Ann-Marie but blame it on our daughter Kristina, without whose bullying, support and encouragement it would not have seen the light of day.

Contents

Introduction .... *iii*

1. Why Was He Born At All? 1
2. Down to the Sea in Ships 8
3. Soldiers in Blue 12
4. Pity about the Natives 17
5. The Exodus Hunt, Mark II 21
6. Then She Went and Caught It at the Astra 25
7. Escape and Evasion 29
8. A Man Who Rides Horses 37
9. No Room at the Inn 39
10. Jordan's Burning 42
11. Per Ardua? No, Quo Vadis? 44
12. Chico Sahib 46
13. The Island of Love 49
14. Timbou 53
15. Soldier's Return 58
16. On Secondary Duties 62
17. Ill Met in Grimsby 65
18. The Great Fire of Manby 67
19. Goodbye Old Soldier 70
20. 'Echo Foxtrot Rolling!' 73
21. Salute... He Moves! 78
22. Kerstin's English Usage 80
23. No Stayin' Power 83

24. Nicosia...88

25. Mixed Missiles 90

26. Mixed Messages 95

27. A Piss Pour Job...98

28. Days of Glory 104

29. A Family at War 112

30. The Foursite Saga 116

31. Up the Slippery Pole 119

32. Somewhere East of Suez 123

33. A Matter of Approach...128

34. Down Under 132

35. An Identity Crisis..136

36. Penang and Babi Tengah.....................................139

37. The Joke Warfare Establishment 142

38. An Old Flame or a Flicker? 146

39. Those Who Can't, Teach 149

40. The Pickle Factory 152

41. Fall Out the Roman Catholics and Jews............160

42. Hit Me Again, I Can Still Hear Him 163

43. Us Bloody Europeans 167

44. Cincafuk 172

45. Santa Lucia..176

46. Sailing By 178

47. They Only Fade Away 185

        Epilogue...*187*

Introduction

I started scribbling down my recollections of the past to relieve the boredom of retirement from the Royal Air Force. If I hoped for more it was that my words might interest and amuse my immediate family and provide for those that follow an insight into our lives and times. Should others read my stories, then I wish no offence to anyone living or dead or to the Service that I loved. With this in mind, I have included the disclaimer and, where possible, have changed the names of friends and colleagues involved in order to preserve their anonymity. Furthermore, to help assuage my embarrassment in allowing a victory of literary ambition over privacy and good sense, I intend to offer a proportion of any royalty proceeds to the Royal Air Force Benevolent Fund.

Autobiographies often lead us from event to event like milestones to the grave; recording what happened, what the writer thought happened, or even wished had happened. What follows is a dip and a dart from present to past as mood and memory took me, restrained only by the thought that my family would be the most avid, if not only readers. They would hear something of their grandparents, of uncles and aunts and of a love story about a young man called Peter and a Swedish girl called Kerstin who lived happily ever after.

"The Hair Force," Mr Trimmings, the aptly named station barber at RAF High Wycombe would say, "is full of Air Marshals, but I am a *Hair* Marshal". Indeed, he was and one who, by special invitation, stood in proud and distinguished company at the funeral of his friend 'Bomber Harris', whose hair he had attended to throughout the Second World War as Harris directed the might of Bomber Command against Nazi Germany.

Well, I was not to be an Air Marshal either, but the Royal Air Force was to be the backdrop for a substantial part of my life, and to this day I dream in uniform and wake up in pyjamas.

1. Why Was He Born At All?

A nineteen-year-old corporal in the RAF Regiment could not have presented much competition to the university graduates who were my fellow candidates on the Air Ministry commissioning board. The panel may have been impressed by my belated attempts to educate myself or by my shiny buttons or high gloss shoes. But I like to think that what clinched it for me was the place of birth shown on my birth certificate in front of them. 'His Majesty's Borstal Institution Portland'. The President summed up their collective view when, with mock gravity, he declared that anyone so disadvantaged at birth deserved a break!

"You can use *things*," my 75-year-old mother volunteered, when we announced the imminent arrival of child number three in five years of marriage.

Stunned and embarrassed and not completely sure even now that we were talking about the same 'things', as such matters were never discussed in our family, I asked why she had waited till I was 30 to address the issue, or should I say prevention of issue, and why she had not taken her own advice – I was, after all, her last and thirteenth child.

I started to wonder how many children she thought would have been enough, three perhaps? But at number thirteen there could be little doubt that I was unwanted. She quickly recovered the situation by saying that each child brought its own love and that no one could have been more loved than me.

This was a good time to quit, blooded but not bowed from an encounter which at a blow had all but destroyed my memories of a pristine family life.

My mother was not a bookish, clever woman but she was shrewd. Her mother was Irish and this showed in her daughter who was very small and had long black hair, which she wore in plaits to her waist. Married at eighteen, she was in India and a mother at nineteen. My father was a big man, clever and self-taught. He started work part time at Lister's Mill Bradford when he was eight, joined the Royal Field Artillery as a man at fourteen, was married at twenty and rose quickly through the ranks to Warrant Officer. He was mentioned in dispatches and was awarded a field commission following action at 'Ramadi' in Mesopotamia. Years later, I was to walk the same ground but for now I was a healthy big baby in a pram in the Dorset sun.

So, in the words of the old ditty: 'Why was he born so beautiful, why was he born at all'. But born I was, at home in the housemaster's house of the Portland Borstal Institution, which was one of several houses lived in during my sojourn in HM Prisons. I remember warm sunny days, red sunsets and pebbles. I imagined the latter to be in some builders yard but it might have been the Chesil Beach, a long causeway connecting Portland to the mainland or Church Ope Cove which was our family playground.

I suspect my safe arrival was tinged with considerable relief because it occurred close on the death of my infant sister Mary who would have been only two or three. I joined my brother Paul who was five and sisters Joan, Pat, Wendy and brother Raymond all under sixteen. I was aware of my older brothers Albert and George and my sister Frances but it was Biddy who featured so prominently in my early life.

Biddy was the eldest sister. When I was born she was twenty one and she was to care for me till I was twelve as she had others before me. She never sought to be my mother but when I think of sore knees or bedtime, of going to school or having fun – it is Biddy who comes to mind. Biddy on the beach, Biddy making clothes, Biddy making me laugh and drying my tears, Biddy at every turn. War broke out shortly after we moved from Portland to Chelmsford, where we stayed during what became known as the 'Phoney War'.

I have vague memories of an air raid siren and the Chamberlain speech and someone leaving the gas cooker on unlit, causing a panic about a gas attack and I can certainly remember in a twilight sky seeing barrage balloons in the distance, but how much is memory and how much is imagined I really do not know. Less dramatically, I remember following Biddy to the grocery shop with my gumboots on the wrong feet and the laughter it caused amongst the shoppers. I remember the excitement of going in a motorcycle side car ridden by Eric Clarke, the husband of my father's niece Mary and I remember seeing the little tanks or 'Bren Gun Carriers' as they were called, going past the house.

Then there was a hotel and a train journey and a taxi and a falling into a snow drift as we made our way to Wakefield in the West Riding of Yorkshire. We stayed in a large Victorian terraced house near Wood's Farm. There was a Mr. Wood and it was a real farm from where milk was delivered from huge urns off a milk cart drawn by a horse. Mr. Wood must have been a very kind fellow because he allowed Paul and me to have the run of his farm on a daily basis and at weekends it was the venue for family picnics. I cannot remember Mister or a Missus Wood, if there was one, but I remember their lovely big dog.

The rich and to me delightful farmyard smells were in marked contrast to the heavy pawl which seemed always to hang over the rest of the city. Even on the sunniest of days, the acrid smell of industry choked the atmosphere. Indeed, summer or winter, rain or snow, we were never free of it. The snow was everywhere in the winter of 1940 and never more beautiful than on the slopping roofs of the red brick houses, on cobbled roads, gathering in drifts in front of the coloured glass porches and on the paving tiles and on the cow sheds and the hay stacks and the ploughs and carts.

I remember Paul taking me to school by the hand in such weather and of falling and cutting my knee on a bottle, but that must have been the following year because I started school in the spring term. Spring, because I was wearing lightweight, silky, cream-coloured clothes designed and made by Biddy from curtain material. The school was close to the gasworks, where the children were mostly from coal mining families, all spoke with broad northern accents and were dressed in brown corduroy trousers, grey flannel shirts and black lace-up boots. That first day in the infants' class was to mark me from the outset. I was 'posh', an outsider and a target.

His name was Cooper and he had been put up to start a fight with me by a boy called Francis. I had been bullied and name-called for an eternity but now I was encircled and there was nowhere to go. It was a warm summer's day; the playground was asphalt – especially laid to destroy bare knees. Cooper lashed out and missed. My Dad had been something of a boxer in his former years and my brothers George and Alby too. Perhaps it was inbred, but from somewhere came a great haymaker of a punch which sent Cooper reeling. Nose bleeding and in tears he withdrew from the contest. In books and films the previously downtrodden victor of such an encounter is invariably carried off shoulder high. Not so with me, but at least after that they left me alone.

Although I was sorry to leave the farm, our next house was big and impressive. Wrought iron railings and a big gate led on to a large porch. A central hall served rooms on either side and a wide open staircase wound round and round past each of the three floors above. The whole was bathed in natural light from a blue glass dome at the very top of the house. So many rooms on so many floors and an extensive cellar made this the biggest house in the world. A vast heating system powered by a coke furnace in the cellar provided hot water and heating for the whole house and each of the score of rooms had a large Victorian fireplace.

The house was on a road called 'Love Lane', which even then sounded pretty incongruous because next door to our house was the main gate of Wakefield Prison! Love Lane was lit by gas lamps and every night the lamplighter would walk past, carrying a long pole with which he would open the lamps and turn up the light. The twenty foot wide prison wall was the boundary of our back garden and attached itself to the back of our house just below the window of 'the nursery', a name given to a huge room shared by Paul and me.

The meagre coke and coal ration meant that most of our meals and activities took place in the kitchen and scullery where the cooking stove was on in all seasons. The fire in one of the front rooms, grandly called the 'drawing room', was lit in the afternoons and my father would read and snooze there for a couple of hours before going back to work. This was also the piano room where I was required to practice. It always seemed to be warm when my father was there and I was in my 'wigwam' (made of car blanket and clothes horse) behind the big leather sofa, but bitterly cold when I had to practice.

There was a big library with lots of books. My father had a passion for cowboy stories and detective yarns, mostly in paperback. However, there were heavier tomes, many about the Great War, but I was captivated by one, a bound copy of *The London Illustrated News* for a period covering the Zulu War. Soon Chief Cetawayo was more familiar to me than Montgomery, Rorkes Drift more real than Dunkirk. Despite this, the war did impinge and soon all family members except Paul, Joan and me were involved and the fear of the telegram boy, so often the harbinger of bad news, gripped us all.

Raymond was the last one to go, not before the air raid which had us all in the cellar and had Raymond spotting through the coal chute. Every time he lifted the lid there was an almighty explosion – mostly, I suspect now, our own anti-aircraft guns – but my father was finally moved to shout out: "Close that bloody lid and get in here *now!*"

Within a couple of years he would be doing the same thing on the Anzio beachhead, where the fire would not be friendly! Dear brother George, more a dad than a brother, would say his final farewell en route for India, or so he thought, only to be captured in Singapore.

Our final move – to a 'little' house at the other end of Love Lane with only fifteen or so rooms – took place during the last year of the war. Behind the house was a steep brick wall and rickety old wooden steps leading to the railway platforms. The trains were clearly visible from our back garden and I remember how they were painted with big white crosses as they carried the wounded soldiers back from the Normandy landings. The walking wounded were dressed in light blue garb. Escorts, Biddy was one, used to travel with them to hospital or to their homes.

Events in Wakefield were punctuated during the War by visits to and from the Bradford aunts. My father had three sisters, Emily, Nellie and Annie. Annie was the black sheep of the family, married several times, hair blue with peroxide; she was a memorable, fun lady. Nellie and Emily were very fond of sweets, then in perilously short supply. Emily's husband owned a butcher's shop in Bradford and most Sundays they would come to us and sometimes we would go to them.

Usually we went to Nellie's. She was comfortably off and used to live close by in a terraced 'back-to-back' house, which meant just that; two rows of houses with a cobbled path between them, where washing would be hung out and children would play. The front steps of the houses were yellowed with stone. There was a front room with an aspidistra in a brass pot, a piano and highly polished wooden furniture with antimacassars on the backs of chairs and sofa. No one was ever allowed in this room except by invitation and then for only one purpose, to sing Wesleyan hymns accompanied on the piano by Nellie. The rest of the time was spent in the back room, kitchen and dining area, listening to the radio or to conversation which my father and his sisters seemed to vie with each other to deliver in the strongest Yorkshire accent.

The war in Europe ended in the spring but it was the atomic bombs which brought the war in the Far East to an end. A letter from a fellow inmate of George was the first intimation that he had died on the 22nd August, seven days after hostilities had ceased but confirmation swiftly followed. Not that it came as a surprise to my mother, who had dreamt about it a month or so earlier and had 'seen' George die on a train.

"Don't be daft lass," Dad had reassured her. "They don't have bloody trains in the jungle!"

But they did and he had died on one as it made its way out of the valley of the River Kwai.

The dreary war years gave way to a cold, austere period in which a tired old nation licked its wounds and an atmosphere of gloom prevailed. At home things were happening of which I was unaware at the time. George, even in captivity, had been at the epicentre of the family and there was still much talk of him: of loss, tragedy and 'if onlys' which the joy of seeing the others return safely did little to assuage. One by one they left again. Joan married her Guardsman, Emily married an RAF doctor, Biddy married a Prison Governor and Paul went to Sandhurst, so that left just Pat and me. But the overarching issue was now my father's health.

At fifty-nine he was diagnosed as having Parkinson's disease. A proud man, he hated the trembling and the excess saliva. He was no longer able to play cards, which had been his passion, or command the attention of an audience. Worse, all his colourful, albeit unlikely, schemes for eventual retirement were at naught; he could work no more.

The basement flat in Hastings was reminiscent of the dingy cellars in Love Lane. The walls were whitewashed, the subterranean windows at the rear barred, whilst the front window faced a flight of concrete steps. There was no natural light in any of the rooms. My father used to walk along the seafront, pitying the holidaymakers facing the stormy weather and say how he felt he should invite them back to our home. I could not imagine anyone wanting to live in that awful place. My mother spent her time wondering what was to become of us. Pat returned to Yorkshire and married, then there was just me.

My short time at Hastings Grammar School flew by. I seemed more popular than hitherto and had discovered a talent for making people laugh. I did a lot of cross-country running, played for the second eleven on the Hastings County Cricket Ground (and was out for a duck), did a lot of non-scholastic things outside school but, sadly, academic work took a back seat and at sixteen I left school bereft of qualifications.

2. Down to the Sea in Ships

Perhaps it had to do with being born on Portland Island or perhaps it was the light from the Royal Sovereign Lightship moored off Hastings that every night lit my room in our new little house with a re-assuring pulse, or maybe it was reading *Treasure Island* – but from the beginning my heart had been set on a career at sea. At twelve, I thoroughly failed the entrance paper for Dartmouth Naval College, doing well in English but achieving the lowest possible marks in Mathematics. My next window of opportunity was to be at seventeen, but fate, in the form of my father's early retirement, intervened. Despite this, I was soon enjoying myself in Dories and Whalers in the Hastings Sea Cadet Corps, which, as things turned out, was the nearest I got to a career at sea.

Not that I was entirely loyal to the sea cadets. Under pressure I was enticed into the Combined Cadet Force at Grammar School and used to parade in khaki with a Royal Sussex Regiment cap badge on Wednesdays, reverting to bell bottoms at weekends. My poor mother, who I had trained to press the navy suit crosswise, with the seven creases representing the seven seas, gave my khaki the same treatment! It took me ages to get out the unwanted creases and I was stuck with the ironing from then on. But perhaps I am being too kind to her memory and this was her intention all along!

My time in the Sea Cadets was not without incident. Firstly, there was the mine. We were called out to stand station over a live mine bobbing up and down three miles or so off the Hastings coast until relieved by the Royal Navy. Late home after a day at sea, my father would not believe my story.

"Kids wouldn't be allowed to guard bloody mines!"

Next day the local newspaper reported the story and he was duly apologetic.

Then there was the visit to Portland, my birthplace. HMS *Osprey* was the submarine base and we spent three days in subs being hunted by frigates and three days in frigates chasing subs. I was allowed to operate the hydroplanes, which control the decent and ascent of the boat. My conversion to submariner was given something of a shock when, a few days later, HMS *Affray* sank in the Channel in mysterious circumstances. Our boat was the *Aurax*, a similar 'A' Class submarine.

The last adventure before returning home started one night on a fishing boat or Motor Fishing Vessel. I was, even then, convinced that the Services give ordinary things like fishing boats highfalutin' names just to abbreviate them. Anyway, the MFV dropped us off two by two in a small dinghy and we came ashore at Lulworth Cove. It was night and our orders were to return to base. This involved a long and quite dangerous route up and down the cliffs and along the shoreline. To make matters worse my companion sprained his ankle, so I had to help him all the way back. Working with the Marines from the same beach many years later reminded me what an achievement this had been.

A poignant memory from that first visit to my birthplace was finding the grave of my little sister. I say 'little' because Mary was only four when she died and it set me wondering whether people grow older in heaven or remain forever the age at which they die, the latter notion more acceptable to the young than the old. My attention was drawn from the uncared-for grave by the approach of a man I took to be a gravedigger. I asked him if he remembered my father. He said little in reply but mimed the dealing of playing cards. A little girl forgotten but an unendearing human foible remembered. I walked away from the grave and up to the top of a nearby slope. There, beneath me, moored in the harbour, was the Home Fleet with the battleship HMS *Vanguard*. In my mind I recall the fleet was lit up and dressed overall but I was young and imagination can play tricks.

My memories of the sea cadets are all good, from launching and pulling up the boats in rough weather to standing off the Hastings coast close to the *Royal Sovereign* lightship – the same ship which illuminated my bedroom every few moments against a background noise of sea swell on shingle.

In the advertisement to join the Fleet Air Arm, the necessary qualifications were minimal. As I filled in the coupon my logic was that once in the Navy, it would not be difficult to become a seaman officer. But the advertisement was an old one and the branch was closed. However, I could fly on similar terms with the RAF and follow in the footsteps of my predecessor as School Clerk at a local secondary school. What the hell? Almost anything would be better than marking time waiting for National Service in the company of the infamous Welsh headmaster for whom I worked.

This meant a visit to the aircrew selection centre at Hornchurch and a series of intelligence and aptitude tests, followed by a medical. With my hypochondria already well established, I was more worried about the medical than anything else. There was no surprise when the President of the Board solemnly told me that I had failed; not, that is, until he told me the reason. 'Polyps up your nose'. Polyps anywhere meant nothing to me but when he added that it was treatable, panic disappeared, to be replaced by cold resolution to get treatment, get back there and pass.

The offending growths were removed in a lunchtime session at the hospital near the school where I worked. Years later, the same operation in the RAF was to involve a week-long hospital stay. On my return to Hornchurch they pronounced me fit but now said that I lacked the necessary aptitude for pilot training. I felt obliged to point out their ineptitude in not saying this in the first place. Overnight their resolution must have faltered because the following day I received a telegram telling me to report for pilot training as soon as I was old enough.

It must have been a worry to my parents because their concern prompted my Auntie Nelly, one of the delightful pair of aunts from Bradford, to pay for a flight in an aircraft from the airfield opposite our house. My sister Pat, now happily married, decided she must come with me and we had enormous fun, so the ruse failed. I was only sixteen but the months flew by till that day when, at seventeen, I made my way to Cardington for kitting up and then to Digby, a grass airfield close to Cranwell.

I can feel the tingle of excitement return as I recall that cold, still morning, when, in my leather boots, flying jacket and helmet, I made my way out to the Tiger Moth with which I was to wrestle for the next ten hours. I climbed up onto the wing and into the rear cockpit, my parachute fitting snugly into the metal bucket seat. A big compass dominated the instrument panel and in my mind's eye I also see the turn and bank indicator, artificial horizon and air-speed indicator. There is also the 'Gosport Tube', a simple pipe through which to communicate with the instructor in front. I can see beyond the instructor's head the fuselage sloping up through the propeller to the sky. I understand why we have to taxi from side to side in order to see where we are going. I feel the rush of air over the windscreen of the open cockpit, the tail skid coming off the ground and at last the airfield in sight as we ease up into the sky, the flaps come up, we are airborne, the earth below a patchwork quilt ... who wants to be a sailor?

Was it poor navigation or disorientation which rendered me lost on take-off? Was it an inability to judge height or a lack of co-ordination which made my attempts at landing a game of chance? Whatever the reasons, my acknowledged ability to handle the aircraft well in flight and in spin and stall recoveries was insufficient to weigh the balance of judgement in my favour. Although it was to be several weeks later before I found out, for the time being my flying career was over and life in the Royal Air Force Regiment beckoned.

3. Soldiers in Blue

The man who impressed me most at Cranwell was a Flying Officer Shaw, who regaled us with stories of Aden, Iraq and Malaya. What had the Royal Air Force to do with such places? Well, the use of air power between the World Wars to control large tracts of territory is fairly well known and produced a crop of quite remarkable aviators. Less is known of the role of RAF ground forces, especially in Iraq and Aden.

There is an old saying attributed to a pilot called Pontius on hearing about Army aviation, that if God had meant the Army to fly He would have painted the sky brown. I suppose a riposte might have been that if He had meant the Air Force to operate armoured cars, He would have painted the ground blue. Anyway, they did, and very effectively. In particular, No II Armoured Car Company in Iraq played a significant part in the defence of Habbaniya and helped in the defeat of its attacker, one Rashid Ali, a Nazi who led a revolt against the British. The same man who inspired the stepfather of Saddam Hussein of latter day fame.

Now Flying Officer Shaw was in the Royal Air Force Regiment – which was formed during the Second World War to defend airfields and which had operated the armoured cars and provided officers and SNCOs to forces of locally recruited Levies in Iraq, Aden and Malaya. His stories were so good that he soon convinced me that, if I were not to fly, the Regiment provided an excellent outlet for my energies.

Of course, the so-called selection board at Cardington thought I was mad when I declared my intention to join the Regiment and offered much more cerebral things for me to do. Having left me three months to labour as an orderly after my ejection from my first flying course, I was not unduly interested in their views. They offered me nothing in the Regiment but a five-year engagement as an airman. The basic training course at Dumfries in Scotland in mid-winter was not a pleasant experience. The cold weather, the icy ropes on the assault course, the sinister instructors, may all have helped me progress as rapidly as I could towards the Officers Mess.

It was, however, the soup incident which became the compulsive force for my eventual elevation to the officer corps. The food at Dumfries was stodgy but good. Imagination played no part at all in food preparation. I for one was delighted one day to find soup on the menu. I believe I had two helpings. Imagine the disgust when we learned that a drunken cook was caught urinating in the soup. Oh yes, it's true – and it was pea soup! They arrested him and he was duly charged but whilst these formalities were taking place the soup was served and we drank it.

I do not know to this day whether it was my performance during basic training or the express wish of the much-maligned selection board, which resulted in me going straight on to the RAF Regiment Depot at Catterick for training as a weapons and fieldcraft instructor. All that can be said was that it was a blessed relief from Dumfries. The other 'students' were all 'old men' from operational squadrons. It was not difficult to shine at most things and soon I was a corporal, not the easiest rank to hold down, and on my new unit – No.16 Light Anti-Aircraft Squadron, at Innsworth in Gloucestershire.

I knew nothing of anti-aircraft guns and not for the last time found myself having to rely on my juniors to survive. Here I had a stroke of luck. The man occupying the bed next to me was an ex-blacksmith. He was Welsh and a man of few words, every one of which was followed or preceded by an obscenity, usually both. He was also on my gun detachment. An expurgated account of our first chat went something like this.

Him: "Think you're going to tell me what to do?"

Me: "Yes."

Him: "What if I refuse?"

Me: (More bravely than I felt) "I will put you on a charge."

Him: "What if I punch you in the face?"

Me: "Well, then I will be in hospital and you will be in the guardroom."

I waited for the punch to fall.

"I like you, you fatherless child engaging in sexual intercourse!" (or words to that effect) was his final outburst.

From then on he was my henchman. Whatever orders I gave were immediately followed up by "...do as the corporal says now." And nobody argued with Taffy. One day, sitting on the lavatory in the 'ablutions', I overheard Taffy and the others talking about me. It was not all bad and finished when Taffy expressed the view that I was 'posh' enough to be an officer. The next day I put in my application and to my surprise soon found myself en route to the Isle of Man to undergo Officer Cadet Training. Perhaps Taffy's influence was more extensive than I imagined.

I remember with considerable clarity staying in the Seaforth Barracks in Liverpool, the grimy walls a testament to its continual use as a transit stop for troops going to Ireland. My father assured me it was exactly the same when he had passed that way before the First World War. I was able to tell him that they still had not cleaned the windows. As we made our way down the gangplank of one of the old relics of a bygone age that plied between Liverpool and Douglas I could not have guessed how my life was going to change before I once again saw the Liver Building come into view.

"Corporal 'olland eh?" said the razor smart little warrant officer.

"Yes," I said, occupying the lonely ground between his years of experience as an airman and what I took to be the academic if not intellectual superiority of my fellow cadets. He sensed my discomfort.

"Never mind sir," he said, which was the first time anyone had called me 'Sir', "'itler was a corporal." To my shame I cannot recall his name but this kind remark later reinforced at a party by his sensitive rendering of the poem 'If' marked him out as one of a kind and remains in my mind to this day.

"We are short of weapons instructors and you have been chosen from a cast of thasands to be one." So said Sergeant Smith as he introduced me to my 'squad'. Now I was determined to get my squad through and spent a good many hours rehearsing them in the barrack room. I was not completely successful. Let one example suffice. It concerned a bespectacled scientist called Harrison whose round, guileless face I can see in my mind's eye as I write. Harrison could not be described as a military person, he was overweight, slow moving and dressed in military accoutrements, he looked absurd. But somehow he managed to keep going up to the final exercise. I taught him the pneumonic GRIT – this stood for Group, Range, Indication and Type of fire. We rehearsed every situation time and time again. "Number one section ... one hundred yards ... bushy top tree ... right of bushy top tree ... rapid ... fire!"

On his final test he led his patrol out into the dusk on the 'Point of Ayr', a flat area of dunes and scrubland. I positioned myself close to him and whispered instructions and advice as we made our way forward, seeking to locate the instructors posing as enemy, whose position we were to attack and destroy. I suppose we must have been fairly close and moving tactically and very quietly when I noticed to our flank a flock of sheep. Suddenly, without any warning and certainly with no prompting from me, Harrison stood up, pointed at the sheep and shouted "Grip ... Gris ... Shit ... Grit!" and then, fired with confidence at stumbling on the right word, continued "Patrol, one hundred yards, top of bushy tree, fix bayonets and charge." We swooped down the hill towards the sheep, screaming like banshees, as a pistol cracked and a Very light burst above us to reveal the full extent of our folly.

The fact that there were no trees, bushy or otherwise, did not escape the notice of the invigilator as he scathingly summed up the exercise but it was the attack on the sheep which excited most comment, hiding as they were at the top of the imaginary tree. Poor Harrison was to fail but by this time my concern for my squad was overtaken by my own plight. The 'educators' felt that I was not up to the mark and only my high score in 'Officer Qualities' (OQs) saved me from disgrace and spared me to take on another squad for yet another thirteen weeks.

I was devastated and convinced that I would never satisfy the education branch of my competence. They reluctantly shared hegemony over us with the RAF Regiment and were described by one of our ageing aircrew cadets as 'a bunch of poofters'.

I remember agreeing to go on a blind date rather than study, on the basis that trying hard did not seem to produce results and blind dates tended not to turn up anyway. 'Gwen' was to change all that.

It is a strange thing but I cannot for the life of me remember what she looked like. I never had a photograph of her. She might have been something magical from this magical island – like the witches we visited in their woodland glade for tea and fortune telling soon after we met. She was more mother than girlfriend. She gave me confidence, support and companionship and, as the weeks rushed by, we grew ever closer. *Conflict of Wings* was the film we saw in a cinema in Douglas the night before she died.

It was Sergeant Smith who sought me out. I was polishing my boots for the 'passing out parade' only two or three days hence. None of my family could make it but Gwen was to be there. That would be enough. Smith had a badly scarred neck, caused when a gas exercise went wrong, that always acted as a barometer for his feelings. On this day it was a livid maroon.

"I've some bad news for you Sir," he said. I expected to hear the worst about my father, who was very ill at the time. He paused. "It's Gwen. She's dead. A burst appendix."

For a moment I could not take it in. Young people like us don't just die, especially not my Gwen. There were no doubt valid excuses why I did not go to her funeral but to tell the truth at the time I did not want to. I wish that I had; it would have been little enough to do for one who had loved me so selflessly.

I am in danger of doing a 'Plodger' here, of whom more much later, but I thought it right to trace my course through those early and formative months which led up to my commission in the RAF Regiment. But I will now leap forward a few months when, after a short stay in Egypt, I would find myself in Iraq. Not with the armoured cars, which had sadly fallen victim to a defence cut, not even with the Levies, although we lived at first in the Levy Mess, but with a regular Light Anti Aircraft Squadron of the RAF Regiment.

4. Pity about the Natives

Smells, not necessarily nasty smells, trigger the memory. If blind-folded and magically transported to another country the location could be identified 'on the nose'. Trying to remember the smell in isolation is a different matter, rather like trying to remember last night's dream or to describe a sneeze. Perhaps it is more than just smell; it may be taste as well. 'Aroma' is probably a better word; it conjures up herbs, perfumes and the sublime as well as filth, mud and the earthy.

Rather like St Joseph, I took a flight into Egypt to a place called Fayid and then to Deversoir located on the Suez Canal close to the Great Bitter Lake and it was there I joined No.26 LAA Squadron as 'A' Flight Commander. I was immediately struck by the inept way the locals were treated. There was a serious military situation as political activists and terrorists tried to evict us from the Canal Zone and a good deal of British blood had been spilt, but to me, somewhat naively, they seemed more sinned against than sinners. Indeed, when first on Orderly Officer Duties, I had to order a doc-tor, senior to me by far, to treat an Egyptian knocked down on the camp in a traffic accident. His leg was broken and bleeding; he might die if he was not treated; he might sue if he was. He did not die, neither did he sue.

Across the canal was a high sand bank and beyond that the Sinai Desert, stretching a hundred miles or so to St Catherine's monas-tery in the Blue Mountains.

Always keen on water, the canal was a great temptation to me, so at the first opportunity I leapt in and splashed about. Towering above me, a troopship went past not twenty yards away. I made my way to the bank – no clothes!

'Clefty Wallahs,' I thought, in my new-found lingo. Then I spot-ted them some considerable distance along the bank and it became clear what had happened. The ship had drawn me along in its wake for many yards. Nobody was much interested in my experience in applied physics but they were astonished at my stupidity in swimming in the canal at all.

Alexandria, Cairo and the pyramids were all out of bounds and I had to content myself with Port Said and Port Suez and the 'Gully Gully men'. These might be described as street magicians. Their dexterity in switching chicks from one part of their anatomy to another was quite extraordinary. The 'three card trick', they were weaned on and you could always be sure they would win any game of 'chance'. I suppose mention should also be made of the *Alakefik* men. These claimed to be disinterested bystanders whose mission in life was to promote the welfare of others. "I'm Alakefik, you want nice clean girl? Persian carpet? Sightseeing tour? Etc..." No doubt their offspring work in PR and advertising now.

First impressions often stay with us forever. The first day the headquarters at Ismailia had to be visited; it was very hot. The next day I was to go to the ranges at Fayid in the early morning. Dead to the world until the 'gharry' (5 ton truck) hooted outside my door I leapt up, trying desperately hard to put on my foxes putties, shorts and shirt all at the same time and terrified of being left behind. To describe the journey as cold would be an understatement. I had braved the worst that Scotland and the Yorkshire moors could throw at me. I had swum the River Swale in flood in March for a dare. Yet, I never felt the cold like that morning in Egypt. Within three hours, with the sun climbing towards its zenith my body began to soak up the heat, a little while later the heat reflected by the white sand was unbearable. Was I to suffer the same torments from the climate that my father did?

"It's like someone opening an oven door," is the way that George William described the heat of 'Mespot'. I remembered these words when the door of the Valetta aircraft let in the first blast of morning heat from the plateau airfield which dominated the huge base at Habbaniya in Iraq. My squadron had been transferred there from Egypt as the bases in the Suez Canal area were closed down. The oven stayed on as we made our way down the dusty road to the main gates of the base and the 'Cut'. The Cut was a canal linking two points of a bend in the Euphrates and the source of a water supply which beyond those huge wrought iron gates created a veritable Garden of Eden.

The metalled roads of the camp were lined by Cypress trees. Rich grass and foliage abounded and a neat tapestry of irrigation ditches took the gentle babbling of water to every corner of this man-made paradise. No Nissen huts and tents here but permanent buildings, houses and churches, the whole creating normality in this wilderness that was anything but normal. There were lots of horses and, to my astonishment, a fully equipped racecourse with totalizer board and grandstand. My first letter home cited two dusty towns, 'Fallujah' and 'Ramadi', well away from this verdant enclave, as points of reference. Our 'Mespot' warrior could not have comprehended this land of milk and honey but he would always remember those two towns.

Sharing the benefits of the Cut was the 'civilian cantonment' in which several thousand Assyrians had settled. Smallholders, traders, servants and levy soldiers, they were part and parcel of this British garrison and owed little if any allegiance to the Iraqi King. They were not alone, indeed, a polyglot of the various peoples which make up the inaptly called Arab Nation called this home. There were Kurds, Palestinians, Assyrians and various creeds and sects with little in common but the search for security and the means to live. From the outset, I felt they were sailing in a fatally flawed vessel.

One of the traders was called 'John the Baptist'. I assume he was a Palestinian. He had a shop in which he sold all manner of jewellery and in particular finely worked items of filigree silver. Many years later I was to see similar work in Amman and buy some for my wife, Kerstin. I recognised the wizened face behind the counter. He said he remembered me from the old days. Perhaps he did, but as I walked away from his shop and saw the sign 'Jean Baptist' under an Arabic scrawl, it was good to know that at least some had survived.

Our first encounter with one of our own was over a late breakfast in the Levy Officers Mess. He was a portly fellow in jodhpurs and riding boots and sported a monocle. His first and, as I recall, only words to us on that occasion were: "I've been chasing donkeys". What we were to make of this, heaven knows. The monocle fell out onto the three-day-old copy of *The Times* he had been reading and with that he got up and walked away. He was the President of the Mess Committee, a bachelor and altogether very odd. His tipple was gin with cocktail onions and his periodic cry in any company was "Nimrod!", who was his long suffering bearer. "Nimrod, I want some more gin on my balls!" What must they have thought of us?

Like Corporal Nimrod, whose colourful name is easy to remember, Rashou, my bearer, was an ex-Levy soldier. He was attentive and loyal and always commanded my respect. I wonder what happened to him and to his kind when we hauled down the flag, and order gave way to tyranny. Pity about the natives.

5.   The Exodus Hunt, Mark II

"You promised me that I could have a dog if I passed my entrance exam to Grammar School and if I passed my music exam."

"I didn't, Ann-Marie, it was your mother".

A mother who, I should add, had such a detestation of dogs that the setting of even seemingly impossible tasks as a condition of acquiring one had not sounded too good an idea at the time.

"It's not fair, you had a dog once, didn't you Dad? Tell her they are great. Go on, tell her!"

Great indeed, mine was a Great Dane. I was a new officer in Iraq and the poor beast had just been abandoned by its owner. We found each other, as they say. It was outside my door one frosty morning and I was foolish enough to let it in. An hour later, Rashou my bearer said: "Dog goes or Rashou goes." Well Rashou stayed and Dog stayed too. He was called Jumbo and his huge gangling gait told me why.

My brother officers somewhat unkindly put up a notice in the Officers Mess of the 5,000 strong Iraq Levy Force which read: *Pilot Officer needs new home, apply Jumbo, Room 35.* However, Jumbo was to help preserve my sanity for many months and it was with a heavy heart that, despatched on an operation to Jordan, I had to leave him behind.

Jumbo joined the group of dogs which had attached themselves to the younger officers of the anti-aircraft wing on which I served. There was Charlie, we called him 'the social dog' because although only a mongrel he found himself at home in any company. His most famous attribute was an ability, or an affliction, I don't know which, to keep his tail still and shake his body.

Charlie used to do other odd things, like falling asleep on top of walls and then falling off. Sadly, he also used to sleep in holes in the road and finally was killed in one by a truck which callously thought that the road belonged to him. Long before this though, he enjoyed his capers with Rusty, described by those that fed him as a

'Rhodesian Ridgeback', with a Saluki called 'Betty', an Alsatian called 'Bofors' and with several others whose names escape me.

It was our practice to tie all the dogs together on one long rope and to avoid whispering "cats", which would send them rushing off into the bush. On this particular evening, dressed in the regulation Red Sea Kit – white shirt, white trousers, bow tie and cummerbund – we approached 'The Club'. Now this was the coolest place in Iraq on a summer evening, sporting roulette wheels and all the fun of a mini Monte Carlo. Little tables and occasional chairs were set out all over the lawn, together with standard lamps and fairy lights. Ladies dressed in pretty frocks and waiters in fezzes added colour to the whole scene.

I can vouch that no one said the forbidden word. Who knows, it might have been a wild dog or a jackal which drew their attention. Whatever it was, the rope was pulled from our hands, the dogs spread out in line and the whole pack hit the lawn of 'The Club'. The devastation had to be seen and heard to be believed: women screaming, lights flying, men cursing, dogs barking, chairs and tables scattering, glasses breaking, until at last, in one great bicycle smash, they wound themselves around a palm tree. The rope parted and the dogs were gone.

A single unruffled voice was heard in the uncanny silence that followed. "Place your bets for the twelfth throw of the evening." We retired unseen into the undergrowth and waited some little while before returning. The place was alive with rumours as to what, or who, had caused the mayhem. There was a regular pack of hounds, which was called the Exodus Hunt; someone suggested it must have been these, less horses and huntsmen and as junior officers it seemed like a good idea to foster.

Jumbo and Bofors were almost my undoing. They got on well enough in the 'hunt' but they did not really like each other. Worse than this, Bofors was an aggressive dog, trained to kill. It was therefore unwise of me to allow Jumbo to invade his territory, for while most of Iraq, from Baghdad to the port of Basra, was Jumbo's to play in, the gun lines belonged to Bofors, perhaps not surprisingly, because that was the name of the guns and Bofors was the mascot.

On this particular winter's morning, I think while Rashou was 'doing' the room, Jumbo came with me to work. It was great fun walking briskly along the Cypress-lined roads flanked with irrigation ditches in this man-made oasis by the Euphrates, to the single-storied buildings that we used for offices. We were only a few yards from my office and safety when, with a snarl, there was Bofors. Now to be fair to Jumbo, he readily backed off and would have taken off for the plateau which dominated the camp, but Bofors caught him. The great sloppy dog let out a pathetic cry and, filled with compassion for my best friend, I stepped in to separate them.

My intervention was successful in that Jumbo was released and, with no thought for his best friend, was gone. Bofors now had his teeth into something much juicier – me. Worse than that, he had hold of a part of my anatomy without which I would have been quite lost. After a moment of agony he let go. I ripped down my trousers, knowing that it was possible to sow limbs – and things – back on and suspecting that the item might have fallen down to the gaiters above my boots. I could see nothing except a great deal of blood. I probed no longer but pulled up my trousers and made for the nearest vehicle. "Take me to the hospital fast!" I said, and Curtis, my CO's driver, kindly obliged.

It was not far to the hospital, just time enough to convince me that this was some form of retribution for my sins and that the life of a celibate monk was all that remained open to me. The large number of medical staff who found it necessary to render assistance and proffer opinions as I fought to discover how much of me was left, heightened the drama of those first moments in 'Casualty'. It was not long before I appreciated that I was some bizarre side-show and soon afterwards I heard the first giggle.

"It really will be as good as new," the doctor assured me, after asking me for the umpteenth time whether it really was a dog that bit me. I was not convinced it had been that good before and, at the time, could not hazard a guess as to what else he thought had bitten me. The wound was soon bound up and I was being comforted by an attractive Assyrian nursing attendant.

The Assyrians are a minority Christian sect in Iraq and very moral. "Don't worry," she said, "I too was bitten there." Despite the shock, I had to laugh. Either she had got it wrong or my future life might be more interesting than I could ever have hoped for! Perhaps it was the nurse that caused the reaction, perhaps it was the bromide wearing off, but what joyous agony I felt as feeling returned.

The CO's wife was the first woman to show a special interest in my recovery. Curtis had apparently seen her moments after he delivered me to the Doc.

"It was terrible," he told her. "Fancy being ravished by a dog." This bloodthirsty monologue went on until at last she said, "Where did the dog bite him then?"

"Right in the c**k," he said, without a moment's hesitation.

The news was soon all over camp but it was the ladies who came to see me. Indeed, for weeks after my release from hospital I was never short of an escort. What happened to the dog? Well, the same friendly types who had announced that Jumbo had adopted me now wrote the following:

'Bofors fights Pilot Officer and gets him in the end'.

In a kinder hand was, 'Dog bites off more than he can chew'.

A third wrote, 'Bofors now a cocker'.

Bofors was allowed to live but, rather like a latter-day Captain Ahab, I kept him at a distance for fear that he would come back for more.

"So, Ann-Marie ... of course I will tell Mum about dogs and what fun it will be to own one again!"

6. Then She Went and Caught It at the Astra

Astra cinemas were supposed to be smoked-filled, dingy places in which old films were allowed to break down to the cheers of an uninhibited audience. The new open-air cinema at Habbaniya was a departure from this general rule. Or was it?

The night was warm but not unpleasant in the huge amphitheatre, Roman in its proportions, under the star-studded canopy of a desert sky. The opening night was attended by a phalanx of air officers and their ladies and their sundry children, together with lesser mortals, many of whom had imbibed, from the several clubs and messes. In short, it was crowded, it was mixed and it was potentially ugly.

The film chosen for this auspicious occasion was so memorable that the name escapes me, indeed I suspect it had by the next day. But the plot is not hard to recall. A young man fell in love with a delightful nymph – she may have been the girl next door – and she with him, clear for all to see but themselves. Misunderstanding dogged their early relationship. Just when the clouds began to lift and they prepared to throw themselves into each other's arms, World War One unkindly intervened.

A date, a battle, another date, another battle, the years turned over in a calendar superimposed on the Somme, Ypres and other scenes of trench warfare. Lines of men, eyes bandaged, gassed and holding onto each other for support. Suddenly, our friend was there in a field hospital and so was she, now a nurse. He sees her upturned face, his heart leaps and then he is plunged into despair as she allows herself to be kissed by another. He turns his head to the wall. She goes off with her brother who has called in to say goodbye on his way to the front and certain death.

The lovers meet again as the same wretched calendar marks off different dates against the raging Spanish civil war.

"You never married then," she says.

"There was only you," he replied, "and when I saw you with your fiancée in the hospital at Uremia Frog..."

"Silly, that was my brother, he bought it the next day!"

"Oh my darl..." A huge explosion rent the air, the attack is on. "Go quickly darling!" he says. "We will soon be together."

Little does he know that she is to lose her memory whilst he hunts for her in China, despite the calendar and several more battles, this time punctuated by screaming Zeros driven by little yellow men with more on their mind than our unfortunates. A bit more calendar and a burst from Winston Churchill finds our two love birds, greyer now and careworn by Max Factor in war-torn London; he returning to his club, she running to a shelter.

Bang! "The shelters cop't it guv," says the typical cockney air raid warden. "It could be dangerous in there." Our hero rushes in and, to his astonishment, lying there covered in blood, is herself. He drags her to safety and sees the joy of recognition in her eyes. He sees too that she is not long for this world.

"Hold me darling," she says.

"I've always loved you," he says. "Don't leave me now."

In the poignant silence and from the bowels of the 'one and nines' an earthy voice cries out, "Get it while it's warm!"

Pandemonium breaks out. The remainder of the dialogue is lost to roars of approval or protest from every side. Distraught parents, embarrassed husbands, giggling wives and rude soldiery competed in the hubbub which brought to a close a noteworthy, if not exactly successful, opening night.

Fast forward many years and *El Cid* was an epic film used, perhaps by a management with memories of Habbaniya, to open the new cinema in Akrotiri. Indoors and of more modest proportions it was a far cry from the Astras of old but plush seats and air conditioning made it a haven in the humid Cyprus summer, the summer when Flight 4025 made its mark on cinema history.

The Flight Engineer shouted to me across the airless corner of a metal hanger which we grandly called the 'Passenger Lounge'.

"We have a very sick aeroplane which is going nowhere tonight." This was not a comment likely to inspire confidence in the breasts of travellers but these were all airmen familiar with the currency of the lingo used.

Soon I was being pressed on all sides by a hundred men irritated by heat and delay and the alternate confines of 'the lounge' and a very hot RAF Britannia aircraft, whose sleek external looks did nothing to relieve the inferno inside. They were all anxious to find cool comfort and entertainment in the nearby Astra cinema.

"Alright," I said, throwing caution to the wind. "At least most of you will be in one place should the aircraft come good."

"No chance of that," the Flight Engineer declared, with all the confidence of the technical autocrat.

"OK," said the Captain about an hour later, "give me the PAX." This does not mean peace, anything but, it simply means passengers, however, by this time I had none of either commodity.

"But your Flight Engineer..."

"That man's a fool," he said. "Let's go or we will be out of crew duty time."

"Fifteen minutes," I said, and started the round-up. A message was broadcast throughout the camp but I made my way to the cinema and *El Cid*.

At this juncture I should perhaps explain that *El Cid* was not about a Dago detective or the Spanish Inquisition but a 14th Century Spanish nobleman who fought the Moors to a standstill on behalf of the King of Spain, who was in no way gratified by his action. There were some compensations. He was, for example, married to Sophia Loren, although he only saw her twice, once to make love and the second time to see his twins. Clearly not a man to do things by halves.

As luck would have it, one of my passengers had been a part-time cine projectionist. I called him to the foyer and scribbled down a message.

"Announce that when you have a moment," I said, as he rushed up the stairs to the projection room. Our friend was not in the waiting business and made his announcement right away, without even glancing at the screen.

El Cid, meanwhile, was about to be banished from the kingdom by Royal Command. This proclamation was to be delivered by a nobleman after a blast on several and many trumpets. There was a suitable pause for dramatic effect, after which the nobleman unwound his parchment and said, "Would the passengers of flight 4025 please report to the Air Terminal for immediate enplanement." This short message coincided exactly with the length of the proclamation and, as he finished, so the parchment was wrapped up and the noble and his team exited stage left.

The laughter went on long after our passengers came tumbling out.

El Cid was not banished in that showing, although not even Sophia Loren noticed the difference. But the event inspired Kerstin and I to see the film the next night and nine months later David was born, giving perhaps less credit to empathy with El Cid than to the old air force ditty 'and then she went and caught it at the Astra.'

7.   Escape and Evasion

The walls of the crusader castle were silhouetted against a dark funnel of starlit Cyprus sky. The castle, which dominates the Kyrenia mountains, is testimony to the passage of crusading armies, whose graffiti remains etched on its walls to this day. Above all, it gives substance to the legendary exploits of Richard the Lionheart and his lady, the Princess Berengaria although thoughts of adventure and romance were far from my mind as I plodded naked around the courtyard, my hands manacled and holding a stone cannonball above my head. Instead, I groaned the ageless cry of prisoners which had echoed around those massive battlements for a millennium: "Why me?"

The reason for my punishment was slipping my handcuffs in a vain attempt to escape. Heaven knows, a naked barefoot man on a mountaintop would have little chance of evading capture, even if a means could be found to penetrate those dark, forbidding walls, guarded at every entrance. Why then had I done it, if not to escape? It hurts being attached by the wrists and herded around in a long line of lurching bodies, pulled this way and that at the whim of a moron. But the real truth was compunction to exercise, a skill taught me by Mr Potter when I was but a boy of ten, in another prison far removed in every way from this ancient keep.

Mr Potter was often in charge of the 'gate' at Wakefield Prison when I collected the bread from the prison bakery. He seemed interested in me and my views, whilst I was interested in his handcuffs. The outcome of this relationship was that I became adept at slipping handcuffs and he gathered material for a book he was writing called 'Inca City', a copy of which was duly presented to me on my last errand. *How good it would be,* I thought, as I plodded around the yard, *if the stuff of books was true and I could remove myself and my fellow prisoners in a trice from this torturous visitation to the middle ages.* But this was cold reality albeit in a make-believe exercise known as 'Escape and Evasion'.

Usually the purpose of Escape and Evasion is to train military personnel, especially aircrew, to escape from the hands of the enemy and avoid recapture. But 'High Peak' was an American Navy and Marine exercise, designed largely to train men to conduct themselves properly under interrogation and, no doubt, to provide their Military Police and Intelligence capturers the opportunity to practice their dark arts. Now because it was an American exercise being conducted in a British Colony, a 'few' Brits – four, I believe – were allowed to participate. The fact that I had to be called from Iraq and out of the safe life of the Levant gives some idea of the rush there was to fill the offered places. The thought of a few days in Cyprus was sufficient to overcome the reservations I might have had.

After a typical American briefing, in which the weaknesses of the American captives in Korea were graphically exposed and we 'guinea pigs' were warned about the dirty tricks which would be played on us to reveal all when (not 'if') we were caught. I was paired off with a Marine called George, from Texas. I seem to remember that he was a rather short, stocky man with fair hair but, cold truth be told, the only thing I can vividly recall is that his water bottle, which he colourfully called his 'canteen', seemed to hold much more than mine. Indeed, as we painfully slogged over the foothills of the Kyrenia Mountains, I became convinced that somehow this bottle was being re-supplied from a mysterious source. In contrast, mine seemed to have sprung a leak in the first mile.

From the moment we were dropped off, we were right to believe we were being pursued by the colony's police force and by soldiers. The search was not confined to the ground, helicopters were much in evidence, so it made sense to move slowly and with great care during the day whilst getting as much rest as possible. Under cover of darkness we would make rapid progress, keeping off the tracks and navigating by compass and the stars.

I recalled another long walk at night when, as sea cadets, we had been dropped at Lulworth Cove from a motor fishing vessel two by two, how my partner on that occasion had hurt his ankle and how I had half carried him back to HMS *Osprey* on Portland Island. No mean feat for a fourteen-year-old, although nobody at the time seemed to think it in any way remarkable. Come to think of it, that jaunt along the cliff tops at night was not much less dangerous than walking in straight lines over the Kyrenia Mountains.

As dusk drew in, the going became more and more difficult until I found myself sliding down a steep slope. I grabbed a little bush and held on until George pulled me up. We sank down on the ground and slept for a few hours. As the dawn light filtered down from the mountaintops we saw, for the first time, how the ground fell away into a deep ravine and that the little bush was all which had stood between me and oblivion. It seemed our strategy had been at fault from the outset. However, we had slept and were rested. Furthermore, because we had fallen behind, the search was concentrated ahead of us. We could now make speedy progress with less chance of being caught.

Of course, walking quickly through arid country is thirsty work. Soon my water bottle was dry and the search for water became as important as speed and ease of movement. It may be that my concern for water was coloured by somewhat lurid stories of the 'water torture' told us by the directing staff at the outset. This torture is fairly self-evident. Thirsty men are shown water being drunk or even poured on to the floor and are promised their fill if they divulge certain information. It seemed to me that one should avoid capture if thirsty.

It was late evening on the second day when we found our first plantation. God could have made it a vineyard but instead it was apricots. It was only when we had gorged ourselves with this ripe and juicy fruit and stuffed more in our packs, that we found water. We drank lustily and then filled our bottles, adding, somewhat pointlessly, water purification tablets – foul-tasting little bomblets of chlorine.

As dusk drew in we reached the bridge. It was several hundred yards long and spanned a deep gorge. All our instincts told us that we should walk down into the valley and not use the bridge. We had made such splendid progress that by now we might well have caught up our pursuers. We watched the bridge for a long time, weighing up our chances of being caught against the difficulties and the time it would take to circumvent it.

We decided to go for it but we would move tactically, one at a time, to a point close to the crossing. We would then sprint across the bridge.

It was bad luck, I suppose, that the detachment of Green Howards had chosen just that place to lie in wait. And even worse luck that they avoided showing themselves until we were both conveniently in place alongside them. But luck had little to do with it. We had made the wrong decision.

"Please surrender quietly gentlemen," said a soft English voice.

"Screw you buddy!" was the Texan's response, before he was sat on. For my part, with water treatment still in mind, I ran down the bridge, drinking the remains of my water bottle: mud, dregs, chlorine and all. But escape was out of the question so I came to a halt and, as I did so, threw up the contents of my stomach – every last apricot. It must have been two months later that I found a mouldy apricot still nestling in a corner of my haversack. I retched then too and have avoided them like the plague ever since.

"Want a cuppa sir?" said the young soldier, showing the kind of compassion, wittingly or otherwise, which one might reasonably expect from a front-line soldier. The warm, sweet tea was like mother's milk to a fractious child. Who knows, that might have been my moment of weakness had they wished to exploit it. But it was to be a short respite before being bundled onto a truck and driven to the castle, where we were made to disembark and walk up the steep road to the entrance. Coming down the road was a Turkish Cypriot policeman and as we passed he uttered "High Peak?", not waiting for an answer before adding, "Better you were a thief!"

We were told to remove all our clothing, which was put in neat little piles that rather reminded me of wartime film sequences of Jews being prepared for those infamous 'showers' that were, in reality, gas chambers. I, for one, began to think that I may never be reunited with my bundle, an impression that was to grow during the next few hours as I gradually lost sight of reality.

We were first made to stand some three feet or so from a wall and with arms outstretched lean against it with only our fingertips touching. The torturer then poured water from one glass to another for the benefit of those who, unlike me, had not sampled the hospitality of the Green Howards. It is always best to think of something diverting when unpleasant things are happening and in my experience imagining something worse and being glad that at least *that* is not happening appeals rather more than picturing green fields and homely faces.

This time, true grit and humour came to the rescue, both inspired by the pansiest pair of pants I have ever seen. The unfortunate man who was foolish enough to be caught wearing them was the only man allowed to keep his pants on. No doubt there was some perverse psychology in this, because the victim was a very powerful-looking man with a great deal of body hair that one associates with virility and strength. This escaped me at the time, I just thought he looked funny, but just when my predicament and level of pain were becoming marginally worse than anything I could readily recall, 'Tarzan', as I had come to regard him, drew especial attention to the incongruity of his situation by falling to the floor against the wall and bursting into tears. I felt suddenly both compassionate and incredibly strong and resilient. *They will not break me*, I thought. And perhaps beneath that thought was another, which was that, even if they did, I would not now be the first to crack. More importantly, I didn't have a hairy chest and flowery knickers!

I next recall being herded into a cell with so many other men that our sweaty naked bodies pressed against one another. There was no ventilation, the smell was awful and the atmosphere claustrophobic. I knew nothing of the psychology of sex and had once before subdued the concern induced by close confinement whilst submerged in a submarine, so the overall effect was rather lost on me, but the sense of panic was all around. I thought of Tarzan and laughed.

The object of the emphasis on nudity was, I believe, to belittle us. This became very clear to me when finally the moment came for the interrogation. The cell was whitewashed, the desk was clear and I could barely make out the features of my examiner behind the light glaring in my eyes.

"You miserable specimen," he said, after an agony of silence. We both knew what he meant but by this time I really didn't care what he thought about my manhood. It was then he caught me off my guard. Pointing at a map, carefully placed so that I could see it, he said. "You can't tell me anything I do not already know. For example, this is where you were dropped." He stabbed his finger at a particular point, whilst keeping his eyes on me. I was pleased to see (and the expression on my face told him so) that he was well off the mark.

Even then I knew that selective jabs and well observed reactions of the kind I had so generously given him would soon reveal the precise spot. Later I was to learn that others caught early in the exercise had been tricked more cruelly into giving information. One, told that his wife was dangerously ill, revealed everything against the promise of a flight to her bedside. Another was told that there had been a mistake; he was to have been an inquisitor and how lucky he had been captured and what a pity if his experiences of the last few hours were to be lost – a short report was required ... and so on. Both these men spent the rest of the exercise in solitary confinement, without food and water, to contemplate the folly of their actions.

Suddenly, it was all over. Or was it? Could I just forget the actual pain and fear that these people had caused me? What if, even now, I had the opportunity to hurt them as they had hurt me? What if, hours earlier, when I was momentarily free of my shackles in the courtyard, I had seized a weapon and killed? Perhaps this was just fanciful nonsense. However, someone else on a similar 'exercise' would kill his tormentor and the uneducated public would never understand.

I could.

The romance of Cyprus, so easily dismissed during those few hectic days, did not escape me altogether. When I finally surrendered to the sleep that had been baying at my heels as I trudged across that inhospitable countryside, threatening to overwhelm me at every unguarded moment, it was between crisp clean sheets in a quiet hotel. The 'Acropole' was a two-storey building made of sandstone blocks, fitting in well with the sun-soaked surrounds in this residential quarter of Nicosia. There was an abundance of red geraniums and pelargoniums, of creeping vine and cooling palms and an uncluttered landscape stretching across sandy planes to slate blue uplands and the Kyrenia Mountains beyond. There was the sound of life-giving trickling water, the dewy smell of flowers and, when I woke in the cool late afternoon, there was Bettina.

I could see her plainly from my room as she swayed to and fro on a garden swing in the courtyard below. Within moments I was washed, shaved and standing before her. Hurried introductions followed, in which I recall she was unselfconscious, her innocent blue eyes framed by the gold of her long blonde hair. Late afternoon became early evening and a small band began to play in the hotel garden. It played 'So In Love are You and I'. Her first few faltering steps, as we danced alone in the blossom-laden twilight were a sure sign that this was as unusual for her as it most certainly was for me. Awkwardness soon gave way to quiet contentment.

So began a week of exploration, fun and romance, which was to repair some of the hurt of the last few days. Kyrenia Castle seemed a different place from the grim edifice I had known. The breathtaking views from the battlements remain with me to this day. Then there was Paphos, Salamis and the great Phoenician port of Famagusta, ringed by ancient walls – so many sights and feelings, which made this, the legendary birthplace of Aphrodite, truly an island of love.

Bettina was the daughter of a colonial police officer.

"My Daddy says there will be a lot of trouble here soon," she said. I could not take it seriously. Not these happy-go-lucky people in this heavenly place, this Eden where it was possible to ski in the morning on the slopes of Trudos and swim in the afternoon in the blue Mediterranean. But time was to prove him right.

We said goodbye on the steps of the hotel.

"I wish you could be with me on my birthday tomorrow," she said, with tears in her eyes.

"How old will you be?" I said, trying hard not to feel ridiculous in front of her parents.

"Seventeen," she said.

At twenty I felt so much older than she.

"Don't worry," I said.

"About what?" her parents' expressions seemed to shout.

They need not have worried. Ours had been an innocent and gentle friendship on this island of love.

The barrel of a machine gun glared down over me from above the barbed wire and sandbag emplacements. I felt the cold steel of my gun in its shoulder holster constrict my chest as I drew in my breath at the shock of it. Could this really be the Acropole Hotel, now turned police post and bristling with guns and grim-faced men?

Yes, just nine months after my trip to paradise I returned to find ugliness and hate. *Eoka Enosis* was now the graffiti on the walls and British blood was on the streets.

8. A Man Who Rides Horses

I became aware at a very early age that my father was an excellent horseman but saw little evidence of it until one day in Wakefield, in a big open field in front of the prison, he rode bareback and managed to make the horse perform tricks I had only ever seen in the circus. I cannot say if it was this that fuelled my enthusiasm for horses, or indeed if I ever had any enthusiasm for them at all, but it nevertheless enabled me at the time to give substance to his tales of 'rough riding' in the Royal Regiment. I suspect that in later life his dealings with horses on the track caused him and his rapidly-expanding family a good deal of grief, so the subject was therefore off the agenda.

I am sure I recall him saying to me that there was a difference between a horseman and a man who rides horses. Even so, the point was dramatically brought home to me on a parade ground in Iraq. The 'A' Flight commander of number one squadron is a very exposed position for a young officer on parade. It was all going rather well until the station commander, fondly known by his troops as 'Black Mac', appeared on a horse, his parade adjutant, also mounted, at his side. From the outset it was evident that Black Mac was going to have difficulty in controlling the animal. It persisted in turning around, to the silent amusement of the entire parade. I say 'silent' because the temptation to laugh on parade is almost overwhelming at the best of times and has to be mightily resisted, especially if you are commanding the most exposed group of revellers.

Biting lips and then cheeks can usually aid resistance and even for the most involuntary gigglers this will normally do the trick. However, on this day Black Mac and his horse together were a test for the most robust, stoic and downright insensitive man on parade; who was no doubt in the back row. The horse, with its hindquarters facing the parade and with Black Mac looking at us over his shoulder, suddenly started to open its bowels, whereupon Black Mac raised himself on his stirrups, somehow seeming to be an extension of the beast. The enormous mound of droppings created seemed like a statement on the proceedings. If it had ended there, perhaps the lip treatment would have sufficed, but the horse then opened its back legs and produced a torrent of urine that threatened to wash away the entire parade. This was too much for all of us. By now, my mouth in shreds and full of blood, I was rocking with laughter and could hear the ranks of men behind me unable to stop themselves from laughing aloud.

The parade adjutant saved the day. He and his horse, in one co-ordinated movement, pranced and distracted us all. He uttered something authoritative to Black Mac and seemed to give him the opportunity to retire purposefully from the scene.

The adjutant was a horseman whereas, even on a good day, Black Mac was not.

Perhaps I should explain that there were two main stables in Habbaniya. One was the Levy Stable, which was run like a unit of the Indian Army. Indeed, its leader, the Levy Force commander, was an ex member of that illustrious breed. He was also the Master of the Exodus Hunt. His wife's name was Pam and I can still hear his cry after sherry in the Levy Officers Mess: "Pam, Gentlemen... To horse!"

The other stable, together with the police stables, was where the other horses stayed. This was known as the Station Stables and if it had a leader I suppose it was Black Mac. As with most other things, competition between the two was rife. It was there that, despite the bizarre behaviour of the rest of the horse riding fraternity, I endeavoured to learn to ride.

My horse, a big Arab stallion, was called 'Silver Prince'. The beast was a gentle giant and put up with all my faults without complaint. Like Black Mac, I was no horseman, but my memories of a morning ride across the plateau with the hot air blowing in my face and hair are enduring. This was followed by an enormous curry lunch, washed down with cold lager. It was then back to sleep it off until early evening and the call of the Officers Club.

9. No Room at the Inn

These salad days were to come to an abrupt end. The arrival of Colonel Nasser to the presidency in Egypt was to throw the Middle East into turmoil. A colleague and I were ordered to visit a fellow squadron in Jordan to be invigilators at a shooting competition. We arrived at RAF Amman, not far from the capital, to be told that there was 'a bit of trouble' and that there was no room for us in the Mess. Assuming the trouble to be domestic we happily went to live in the Continental Hotel.

My companion, a thrifty Scot, had only weeks before shared a room with me for all of five minutes in the luxury of the Sinbad Hotel in Baghdad before he discovered the price and moved us post haste to the YMCA. So for us, the idea of a free hotel was something not to be missed. The following day we saw from the window that an exercise was going on in the streets. As military tacticians we felt we really must go and see what was afoot.

"My God," he said, as we strode out towards the souk, "You can't fault them on realism!"

But it suddenly became very clear that the bodies in the street were just that. We were walking into an uprising of some kind. I imagine two Luftwaffe officers on a London street at the height of the Blitz might have generated the same kind of stunned reaction that we encountered. We turned about as if on parade and retraced our steps towards the hotel as calmly as we could. An Arab policeman broke the spell. Running forward, he drew his revolver and ordered a wisely parked taxi driver to take us out of town and up to the camp.

"La, La," said the man, which simply means 'No'.

The policeman pointed his gun at the man's head and, as the first stones struck the car, we sped away to safety.

Not that my chum was prepared to stay up at the camp and leave his, and my, precious belongings in the hotel. The moment it was dark we hired a taxi and returned, through eerily silent streets, to the city. We spent a restless night and left at dawn the following day

– the day that General Glubb Pasha was overthrown and the Arab legion turned on its own officers. We flew back to Iraq with some of the stretcher patients wounded in the affair. We were quick to tell everyone of our experiences and were frankly amazed at their total indifference.

I should say that at this particular point in time I was commanding my squadron – somewhat unusual for such a junior officer. A few days after we returned I was woken at daybreak by my wing commander. He was a smooth and articulate man, tall with a slight stoop and had spent his early years in the Brigade of Guards. His pencil moustache accentuated his grin when he told me that, despite being the youngest squadron commander in the Royal Air Force, I might soon be the most experienced. We were to go to Jordan to protect British lives and property.

"It's started up again," I said, assuming the worst.

Three days of waiting, at one hour's notice to leave, covered in camouflage cream and briefed to fight our way from the aircraft, did little to bolster our sagging nerves. Then, suddenly, the word came through and a stream of aircraft made off in the night towards Jordan, my team leading. We flew over the city of Amman and approached the runway. We were tense but outside everything seemed normal. We landed and made our way to dispersal, where the fire trucks, ground equipment and reception buses indicated that there would be no need to fight our way off the aircraft. Anticlimax, tinged with relief, set in.

We remained seated, our black faces still grim. The aircraft door opened and in strode a young officer in best uniform, wearing a big red armband with a brass crown and eagle. He looked absolutely resplendent, in total contrast to us.

"Welcome to Royal Air Force Amman, where the time is 2200 hours," the apparition said. He went on to tell us what arrangements had been made for our accommodation and transportation.

"Wait a minute," I said. "What about the trouble?"

Without batting an eyelid he said, "Oh, all that happened last week."

Was it a cock-up, or part of some devilish plan yet to unfold? I could not say. We featured, somewhat unfavourably, on Egyptian radio broadcasting to the Arab World and were soon dispatched into the desert to Mafraq, where there was a huge runway, a Nissen hut and nothing else. King Hussein survived and instead his cousin, King Feisal of Iraq, was later to fall victim to a bloody revolt.

As for me... well the experience told me at least one thing. It would be nice to be like that chap with the red armband – a Movements Officer.

Little was I to know what fate had in store for me.

For the time being there was only Mafraq and mud, with the odd invitation to Amman; once to the Embassy and once only to the Officers Mess. On neither occasion did I acquit myself very well.

I still have the invitation which invited me to drinks on Her Majesty's birthday. I strode through the door of the Embassy to be greeted by a dapper little man who extended his arm on which, taking him to be a flunkey, I promptly hung my coat. The pained and chilling look Her Most Britannic Majesty's Ambassador gave me as he passed on the coat to one of his staff and proffered his hand to the next guest is all I can remember of that evening.

The interesting thing about the visit to the Mess at Amman was that it never actually took place. It was my wily Scottish friend's fault.

"We cannot just ignore them," he said, as we spotted three of his sergeants just going to a bar and beckoning vigorously to us. Now in those days my drink was gin and tonic.

"Well," he said, after we had downed the first drink, "time to go. Mr Holland and I are guests tonight up at the camp."

I have a vague memory of going into the bathroom of the house where we were to change. There is a more distinct recollection of the lady of the house waking me up from my naked slumber on the bathroom floor in the middle of the night.

10. Jordan's Burning

A dry, hot dust swirled around the tent lines that Saturday morning, the sun soaked canvas reflecting the dazzling whiteness of the desert sky, a throne for the sun god who, even at this hour, dominated all with the searing heat of his withering rays. Twenty miles away at Ramtha, a battered old 'Chevy' was coughing its way across the fields of newly cut maize and corn. This was at the very heart of Jordan's only grain-producing area. The vehicle spluttered to a halt, smoke pouring from the engine.

What happened next can only be conjecture, but the blackened skeleton of the car, its bonnet open, told its own story: the engine fire, the burning, running, dripping liquids; the stubble at the track's edge, the driver's 'inshallah' and idle pragmatism quickly giving way to blind panic as the fire spread from stubble to bales of corn.

The message from the British Embassy in Amman was admirably short and to the point. A request from the King for help to put out a fire was sanctioned and a map reference was given. The duty officer and twenty men should do it. Take blankets and spades, there was no water. The duty officer was me. Within minutes we were heading for Ramtha – at least a hundred volunteers prepared for anything to quell the crushing boredom of the day.

The fire had taken hold over a wide area when we reached our destination and it was some time before we could establish a firebreak in what looked like a moving sea of cut corn topped by orange spume. Indeed, when we damped down the blaze in one place and turned our attention elsewhere for a moment, it would flare up again, threatening to cut teams off. There was only one thing to do, we must advance in line. A small party provided a mobile reserve to suppress any small fires that rekindled in this oven atmosphere.

It all worked out very well and soon the worthy citizens of Ramtha, under their *mutasarrif* or whatever, were urging us to sit down to Arab hospitality. I cannot remember now whether my refusal of their invitation was born of anxiety for the behaviour of my men if the *arak* flowed or the absence of orders covering the situation. Most probably it was dread that, as the guest of honour, I would be expected to eat the eyeballs of at least one of the succulent goats that would doubtless be our reward. My decision was no doubt right but it has robbed my story of a more colourful end.

The King was delighted with our work. The whole area was politically unstable and the villagers had recently been penalized for having befriended themselves with their Syrian neighbours. It seems that the appeal to the King and our success in tackling the blaze restored their flagging loyalty and was a good deal more successful, the Embassy reported, in persuading hearts and minds than the stationing of a battalion of Arab Legion soldiers on their doorstep.

No medals or insignias were to result from this escapade but there was to be recognition of sorts. That evening, the collection of Nissen huts that served us as an Officers' Mess rang out to a new adaptation of the old song 'London's Burning'. It went something like this:

> *Jordan's burning, Jordan's burning,*
> *Send for Holland, send for Holland.*
> *Fire! Fire!*

And so on... To this day I am a bag of nerves if there is rubbish to be burned in the garden. In my mind's eye I see again that rippling holocaust and take the most elaborate precautions, which normally result in my pyre going out before it even starts. As to the event itself, well, long after leaving the Service I visited the RAF Regiment Museum. There, writ large in the short annals of the Squadron was 'The Great Fire of Jordan'.

11. Per Ardua? No, Quo Vadis?

The RAF Regiment motto is *Per Ardua* (through hardship), the latter part of the RAF motto *Ad Astra* (to the stars) is left off. This was, I always assumed, because we did not fly. On reflection, the promise of hardship without a destination is not much of a motto. One of the wags on my unit felt that our record of movement around the Middle East justified a change of the motto to *Quo Vadis?* (wither goest thou?). We certainly never knew.

Mafraq in 1954 was little more than a huge stretch of concrete from which Britain, with nuclear air power, could protect its vast oil interests and influence events over the whole Middle East. It added to the encirclement of the Soviet Union and provided a *pied à terre* for the rapid reinforcement of the Far East. Egyptian nationalism was at its height and this, coupled with the never-ending search for Arab unity after their humiliation at the hands of the Israelis, was to be the catalyst for change.

Our arrival from Iraq at this godforsaken spot was a far cry from our flight from Egypt into the lushness of Habbaniya eighteen months earlier. The relief and the anti-climax we had felt when not called upon to fight were compounded by a sense of embarrassment that, somehow, our being there was all a big mistake. Nobody bothered to enlighten or encourage us. Besides, we had left our anti-aircraft guns in Iraq and even when they arrived it was without their ammunition. I should add that a 40mm gun is a very formidable weapon with which to engage targets on the ground as well as in the air and no potential enemy would believe we could be daft enough to have no ammunition.

I took every opportunity to keep mobile and occupied with forays into the desert but, for all that, it was a miserable time. My 21st birthday was spent at Mafraq. A telegram from my sister Wendy arrived, barely decipherable and goodness knows by what route. I still have it. My fellow officers did their best to dispel my gloom. There was something of a party that evening and the presentation of a graph chronicling my relationship with a certain young lady. A few verses of 'Jordan's Burning' and I had had enough.

I walked alone the two miles from the 'Mess' to my tent on the other side of the 'concrete strip', pausing only to respond to the salutation of a passing Nomad. I found my telegram and clung to it like a small boy with his 'teddy'.

I had never felt so homesick.

12. Chico Sahib

The trouble with nicknames is that they are usually fairly apt and it is sometimes difficult to separate them from name-calling. The Nobby's, Taffys and Paddys of this world are luckier than the Fattys and the Gingers. A name like Holland should have produced a solid 'Dutchie', but at school my shape spawned the name 'Fatso'. The pain that this caused me beggars description and, like the 'ugly duckling' I was the last to recognise the metamorphosis as flabby juvenile became lean and muscular youth. It left me with an aversion to nicknames which remains to this day.

It was shortly after my Wing arrived in Jordan that the new Squadron Commander arrived and I relinquished command to him. As you will hear later, his name was rich in possibilities for the teaser, especially as he was not universally popular with the troops. It seemed like a good idea at the time to make myself and as many of my men as I could, scarce. An opportunity arose for us to go along with a colleague on what was for me a 'jolly' into the desert. A great deal of beer and huge blocks of ice were loaded and we ventured forth.

Eric Lock, was the worthy in question. True to his name, his lips were sealed as to where we were going and what we were about. A day in the back of a Land Rover in intense heat found me on the Jordan/Iraq frontier, where we camped – on a disused airstrip, on a disused pipeline station, on a disused pipeline. This was the pipeline that, until the Arab/Israeli war in 1947, had pumped fuel from Iraq to the great oil terminals at Hiafa. This and similar stations were known by a number, prefixed by the letter 'H'.

We all had plenty to eat and drink and then settled down to sleep in a large, unlit aircraft hangar. Most people slept on the floor on camp beds but I slept on the roof of a vehicle, much to the amusement of the others. It must have been in the early hours when, no doubt due to bladders excited by alcohol and the cold night air, the first man got up to go and the first match was struck. I was woken by the shouts, if not screams, of my fellows as they panicked to get up off the floor and onto the vehicles.

In the eerie flicker of an increasing number of paraffin lamps the floor was revealed as a sea of camel spiders and scorpions; it really was the most horrible, bloodcurdling sight. The spiders were as big as a hand; indeed, as the years have gone by I think they may have been as big as saucepans! Some men had the presence of mind to shake their blankets, others were themselves shaking too much for cogent thought but everyone was unnerved by the experience and few slept more that night.

The morning revealed a handful of dead spiders but little more evidence of the terrors of the night. I found Eric in the back of a Land Rover; he was very warm and slightly delirious. My first thought was that he had been bitten by one of these creatures but there was no evidence of that. We put him in the shade and I had the medical orderly take his temperature. The mercury rose to an astonishing 106°F. He should be dead already. What could be done to cool him down quickly? Of course, the ice blocks! What was left of them was quickly put in a large metal tub and Eric was put in too. "Christ that's cold!" he said, in his first piece of intelligible conversation of the day. We watched, fascinated, as his temperature plummeted.

"Allo Allo," replied a dozen voices from one end of the pipeline telephone to the other. Vaguely surprised to hear anything, I held out for Mafraq and persisted until they got me an RAF Officer. "Get an aircraft down to me straight away for a medevac", I said, before the line went dead on me.

Eric, still in the tub, was now chattering with the cold and speaking very quickly, like a gramophone record played at speed. He made a little more sense than hitherto but when I asked him what we were doing there he giggled and said he wasn't sure about me but he was having a bath. I decided he needed more fluids, so he was obliged to drink a great deal of rather tepid water. He didn't like that overmuch and stopped giggling. In fact, he began to look quite green and out of place in the desert surroundings.

The Anson rumbled along the airstrip and came to a halt. Within minutes it was airborne again with the casualty, now mercifully removed from the bath and wrapped in several blankets. The excitement over, there seemed little to do but wait. I occupied myself for an hour or so chasing a desert fox and shooting at it with a .303 Lee Enfield. Whilst I have always dismissed stories that foxes actually enjoy being hunted, I believe this one did. Perhaps he saw from the outset that my shooting was so poor he was more likely to be run down by my Land Rover than shot – and he knew the desert.

It was as I finally gave the fox best that I saw the dust of a dozen huge vehicles, in line abreast, bearing down on me at considerable speed. They passed by on towards the camp, pursued by an RAF Land Rover in which a dishevelled RAF Flying Officer did his utmost to catch up. The handover was nothing if not brief.

"These lorries are full of high explosive bombs. The drivers are Iraqi civilians. They are all yours. Goodbye."

So began for me a series of convoy runs from Mafraq to Habbaniya, back and forth across the Black Desert – a vast scattering of volcanic rocks and one of the hottest places on Earth. I learned the necessary orders and delivered them in Arabic and insisted on the highest standards of safety and discipline from these street Arabs, to whom any kind of order was alien.

They responded by giving me a name which I thought at the time was hurtful – *Chiko Sahib* – and my men and fellow officers quickly picked it up. I became 'Chico Holland'. Still, my father had been called Laddie Holland and he didn't mind it a bit. And it was a lot better than 'Fatso'.

Oh yes, Eric Lock. When I visited him in hospital he thanked me profusely for saving his life but pride in my medical prowess was short-lived. As I left the hospital I asked what had been diagnosed.

"Double pneumonia and gastro-enteritis," was the medic's reply.

I was careful not to enquire further as to which had been his worst enemy: the bath, the drinking water or his second in command!

13. The Island of Love

The opportunity to go to Cyprus again came out of the blue. In command of an independent flight, I was to have the help of a young sergeant whose name was Henty Dodd (soon to become TV personality Simon Dee). We were to be attached to the most famous squadron in the RAF Regiment, No II Squadron. With their emblem of a flying wheel they had grown out of No II Armoured Car Company, which had helped keep the peace on the ground in Iraq between the First and Second World Wars. We were to be used for 'internal security', whatever that meant. All was excitement as we flew out aboard a couple of Hastings aircraft. Their Hercules engines could not grab the air fast enough to propel us on our way to my beloved Cyprus and away from that turgid hell hole.

We were not trained for the Internal Security (IS) role. I had spent several nights with the men, pretending we were on patrol in a town. That is not easy in the middle of the desert but to have gone into one of the Arab villages might well have caused the very situation we were training to prevent. It was fortunate that when we arrived in Cyprus the level of terrorist activity was mercifully low and what patrolling there was, was mostly commanded by NCOs. Indeed, I found myself at a loose end – but not for long. As for my independence, it seemed only a moment before my wing commander from Jordan joined me. He was a new man whom I had never met.

Of course this was all very secret at the time but he told me we were to become an advance party for the rest of the unit. Our role was to support the French paratroopers who were to join the British in that dubious scheme to re-occupy and protect the Suez Canal. We were to go out into the wilderness and prepare to receive our allies. Timbou was the name of this particular wilderness. It was a bit like Mafraq on a good day. The ground was dusty rock and only one Nissen hut graced the skyline. My boss and I, together with a party of half a dozen or so men, came to look and determine what was needed. The answer was easy; everything.

We spent that first night in the hut. It must have been close to dawn when the bullets strafed us. Fortunately we were all lying down and no one was hurt. After some confusion we left the hut and grouped together outside. My instincts were to remain still and observe but my new commander – who did nothing to dispel the rumour that he had served with the 'Chindits' – was not having any of that. I was to take a 'fighting patrol', as he called it, and circle around the hut to look for the enemy.

I might have given him an argument if I had thought for one moment that there was anyone still out there, but I was pretty sure that we had been attacked by a gunman in a passing car, so off I went with three men, all armed to the teeth. We did what we were asked, keeping close to the ground all the time and moving tactically. Suddenly, when we had almost completed our circuit, we saw something move ahead. The safety catches were eased off as the figures began to emerge in the dawn light.

We were absolutely still as I began to take aim at the leader but there was something familiar about his shape and outline which made me pause. Just as well I did. I called out a challenge and up stood my master. It seems he thought it a good scheme to go round the other way! I am sure that, with his experience, he would have seen the situation differently and no doubt watched us throughout our exercise in fieldcraft, but at the time my feeling was that with commanders like this, did we need enemies?

I can see him now, a rather squat figure with thick black hair which protruded from every possible opening in his khaki drills. His chest was frequently exposed because he was constantly rubbing and scratching it – and indeed every other part of his body. Every discussion was punctuated with clawing; sometimes it was a soothing paw, but usually it was a vigorous two-handed exercise at the extremities of his trunk; one hand behind his back whilst the other attacked his crotch. The more agitated he became the more he itched and the more he scratched. Hopefully, this was a temporary aberration, but if it was a stratagem to distract his audience, it worked. Fearful that he would go into a frenzied spasm, I would concede any point and retire, feeling decidedly itchy myself.

After this contretemps with the friend within and the enemy without, we returned to Nicosia, where the airfield was simply groaning with aircraft of every kind, with the famous Canberra predominating. Lines and lines of tents and temporary toilets and washhouses stretched right down to the perimeter track. This was indeed a logistical nightmare of enormous proportions, which should have given me a good deal of sympathy with the quartermaster I was to see that morning. In the event, it didn't.

One hundred five-man tents, five hundred camp beds, the list of our needs was unfolded before the quartermaster. His response was abrupt.

"You will just have to sleep under the stars and suffer a little." It was very clear to me that this large, fat man, who oozed sweat despite the electric fans he had positioned on every available flat surface in his office, had suffered nothing worse than a cold shower. Knowing that my scratchy friend had been called to see the Commander in Chief, I asked casually, "May I use your phone?"

"Of course, old boy," he replied.

"Give me the C-in-C's office," I said into the receiver. Before I could say more, the phone was grabbed from my hands.

"Alright, alright," he said. "You don't have to make a fuss. Things are very difficult you know..."

As my trucks were loaded with everything I needed and a bit more for good measure, I took off in the direction of the Officers Mess. Covered from head to puttees with fine dust, I must have looked a sight. The bar was heaving with people, mostly aircrew from the bomber squadrons. Suddenly there was a familiar face; she was a Russian interpreter so I was hardly surprised to see her in this, the 'listening post' of the Middle East.

She had been the roommate of the young lady whose activities had been so well chronicled by my fellow officers for my 21st birthday. Maybe she had been entertained by her friend's stories of torrid nights beneath the palms but, whatever the reason, the fact that it was lunchtime mattered not a bit as we wandered off to claim one of the many tents. We sat on the bed for no more than a moment before the tent flap was thrown back and a dapper little man in a silk dressing gown came in.

"I say, I am frightfully sorry," he said, twitching his moustache. "I thought this was *my* tent."

It was. As he left through one flap to double check, we made good our escape through the other.

It was one of those days!

14. Timbou

Once back at Timbou with my spoils, the next problem was to erect the tents on the rock-hard ground. We succeeded only with the help of the Royal Engineers, who came to the rescue. It was they, also, who dug us deep pits for use as latrines and waste. I have noticed that camp lavatory stories abound in all the best novels, so, as mine are true, why not here?

I suppose we had been established at Timbou for about a month before the RAF proper joined us. Clerks and mechanics, cooks and medics, they really were unprepared for field conditions. As 'Camp Commandant', a title imposed on me by my scratchy friend, I was very concerned lest we fall victim to the dysentery that was at epidemic proportions in some camps on the island, particularly at Nicosia. It was most important that all cooking utensils, cutlery and mess tins were kept clean. My instructions to the cooks were simple. They were to sprinkle a few drops of petrol into the waste pit every evening to help stop the flies from breeding.

The explosion rocked the camp and a yellow fireball, followed by licking tongues of flame, hovered over the tent-lines. I rushed to the scene, my revolver at the ready. I could see the dark silhouettes of four men, close up to and seemingly transfixed by, the darting flames. My first thought was that this was a strange place to put a bomb but when I reached the scene the men were dressed in cooks clothing. They were bedraggled, smoke-streaked and devoid of facial hair. Without eyebrows or lashes their faces were like orange moons in the flickering light.

"What happened?" I demanded, glad to see that they were alright but with anxiety turning to irritation at the realisation that this was self-inflicted and was somehow going to be put at my door.

"It must have been the petrol you told us to put on Sir," one said, confirming my worst suspicions.

"How much did you sprinkle?"

"Only a jerrican full (4.5 gallons!)," was the answer.

I never did discover why they lit it.

Daylight revealed the full extent of their bombardment on my new tent-lines. For about 100 yards from the pit the area had received a rainfall of cabbage leaves, mangled carrots and a great custard of unidentifiable semi-putrid foodstuffs.

"*Quel domage*," said one of the Frenchmen.

"'alf a crown," replied one of the cooks.

The latrine pits served washing cubicles and 'thunder boxes'. It must have been only days after the artillery action by the cooks that I noticed a group of men pulling on a rope which was apparently attached to something in a pit. My curiosity was aroused and as I walked slowly across to them, what appeared to be a large brown sack flopped over the lip. Then the sack twitched and sat up. The man, for so it proved to be, was covered in filth from head to toe.

"How did he fall in?" was my first question.

"He didn't," came a chorus of replies. The rope around his waist proof positive that he had been lowered.

"He was looking for his false teeth Sir," was the explanation.

My sojourn in Cyprus was punctuated by a visit to see my brother Paul in Limassol. My mother had written to say that he was coming out on the aircraft carrier HMS *Ocean*. I was very excited at the prospect of seeing him again and knew that from the date of the letter he had probably already arrived. I rang Famagusta docks and asked if Paul Holland had come out of the *Ocean*. For one moment I had a flashback. There was Paul sitting at the table with a particularly superior look on his face. My sister Joan was annoying me beyond endurance. There was the salad bowl of lettuce and tomatoes swimming in mayonnaise. Joan was a girl and, no matter how irritating, could not be attacked – but Paul had no such immunity.

"Why did you do that?" he was saying, superiority giving way to shock as the salad settled on his head and the sauce ran down his face.

I could not restrain a giggle at the memory of it.

"We are very busy here and have no time for..." I put down the phone and rang Limassol docks, careful this time to say 'HMS Ocean'. Paul had disembarked that very moment and spoke at once on the phone. We hastily agreed a meeting place and a few days later I walked up to his camp, on my own and armed with a Smith and Wesson revolver. Shock at my lack of concern for my personal safety soon gave way to amused curiosity about the age and nature of my sidearm.

Paul's colonel seemed a very amiable man and when he invited my opinions about officers of my regiment who had been formerly in the Indian Army, I happily volunteered them. I really could not understand why Paul was kicking me under the table as I recounted stories of the Indian Army 'Blimps' I had met. He suddenly asked after someone very well known to me and I could scarcely hide my surprise as – partly from a misplaced sense of loyalty and partly because I had a dreadful premonition of what was to come – I tried to exclude a recent commanding officer from the rest of the ex-Indian Army officers I had known. Unconvinced by my efforts to dig myself out of the chasm into which I had slipped, he went on, "Edward and I went through Sandhurst together and joined the Indian Army on the same day."

Paul likes to tease me that I blighted his career from that day forth but somehow I think not even the Indian Army would do you down for having an idiot in the family!

The invasion of Egypt came to a sudden end. We were not to return there for me to complete the cycle started three years earlier, when I had first stepped off the plane at Fayid and taken my first breath of that unmistakable Egyptian air. The nature of the cessation of hostilities and the whole escapade were to scar British politics for a decade. I felt from the outset that it was wrong to invade Egypt and, for the first time, questioned the morality of our actions and of being an, albeit very small, military pawn in a game played out on the world stage.

With only two nights to go before returning to the UK, I was asked to sign the 'bath run' authority to take the chaps to nearby Ayious Nichalious. "Make sure the driver stays off the beer," was my only instruction to the sergeant in charge of the party. He was a young and popular man and natural leader, whose wife and young family were in England. He could be trusted to look after the others.

A terrible crashing noise woke me from my slumbers, followed by an eerie silence; then came the shouts and cries. The truck was upside down, having rolled through and along the barbed wire perimeter fence, dragging its human cargo with it. Everyone I saw seemed to be oozing blood. I do not know why I chose this particular young man to look after – I'll call him 'Mac' – maybe he was the first one that I came to. The mind mercifully blocks out the detail but it leaves flashbacks of both sight and sound. In one I am holding Mac, who is horribly injured. He is conscious and I am telling him he will be all right. The next is of a doctor leaping from one recumbent form to another. He pauses for a minute. "He's dead," he says, in a matter of fact way, before striding off. I knew he was not dead but understood the doctor's dilemma. Why should he waste time on the dying when there were others who could be saved? But Mac heard it too. Before I could properly focus my hatred and frustration on the doctor, Mac's glassy, empty eyes told me that he had succumbed to the inevitable. He was nineteen years old and his young face still stares out at me from a fading photograph of happier times.

The sergeant and the driver were also killed and all the others were injured in some way. Many had been with me from the outset in Egypt. How did it happen? Apparently the vehicle was forced off the road by a private car travelling at speed with its headlights full on. Was it terrorism or just bad luck that the truck hit a bollard? It gave us some grim satisfaction to believe it was the former. It is better to die at the hands of a merciless terrorist than an inept driver. It offers the prospect of revenge and a further twist in the spiral of violence. It allows us to vent our feelings for the moment and gives us courage to suppress our human dignity when we next have the upper hand.

I looked at the bodies on the cold slab in the mortuary and identified them. Minutes before, as they were cleaned and prepared, I stood aghast at the indignities of death. They were the first dead people I had ever seen who were known to me; I felt tired and drained of emotion, an automaton separated from humankind and carrying a terrible weight of guilt. Guilt that I was alive – if indeed this was living – and that they were dead.

On the way back from the military hospital my driver took the truck the wrong way around a traffic island and came to rest, bumper-to-bumper with a private car. People crowded around us and a huge traffic jam built up. This was the moment that the RAF chose to distribute leaflets from the air as part of their psychological operations against EOKA, the Greek Cypriot terrorist organisation. The drone of the aircraft engines was still in my ears when the first crude leaflets fell and were quickly gathered up by the crowd.

The vehicle had an opening in the cab roof where I stood, Sten gun in my hand. I wanted them to attack me. I wanted to let off that gun. I wanted them to suffer and for my own safety I cared not at all. Perhaps it was my grim young face in this indefensible situation which amused them and turned threats and jeers to laughter. I will never know but all of a sudden everything changed and as we were busied and guided out of the predicament I was reminded that these were ordinary people, quick to laughter and slow to anger. God forgive me! The rage had been in me. Now I was back in the human race.

It was a long way home in a Beverley aircraft which stopped at every possible place in the Middle East and in Southern France before a long haul up across the Massive Central to Lyneham, England and home. *Quo Vadis* indeed.

15. Soldier's Return

It seems that despite looking back over a very healthy life, I have always suffered agonies over imagined ailments and diseases. Perhaps the first time I remember being scared of anything in particular was in the old cellars in Wakefield. These covered the whole area of an enormous four-storey house. Each room of the main house was replicated below ground level and were no doubt originally used to provide servants quarters, as well as kitchen, food store, wine cellar and a huge meat preparation room, complete with suspended meat hooks, large stone table and slab.

It proved a useful air raid shelter in the early part of the war and I can still recall seeing my brother Raymond lifting the metal plate on the coal chute to watch the activity outside and above. Every time he did so there would be a gigantic explosion. Whether this was enemy action or the local anti-aircraft battery I cannot say, but it was sufficient to convince us all that Raymond was personally responsible!

But it was not the air-raids which frightened me – although to this day the wailing of air raid sirens still makes my stomach churn – it was, of all things, a piece of rotting wood. I had been playing with it for some time in the gloom and had not noticed it was full of woodworm. My brother Paul came to tell me that we were to go to Sunday School at the old parish church. When he saw the wood he pretended to be alarmed and asked if I had touched it. He then suggested that whatever the wood was suffering from would, as like as not, transfer itself to me.

I remember the misery of that Sunday service, during which I alternated between praying and carefully examining my hands and arms for the tell-tale little holes that would indicate the onset of 'woodworm'! I noticed pores for the first time and the more I looked at them the bigger they got and the harder I prayed. My prayers were answered because by the following day it was clear that I had not contracted the disease.

It was shortly after the war that my sister Wendy, who was in nursing, came home from the RAF and began work in a ward in which people had 'consumption'. I should remind the reader that in those days tuberculosis was still a very potent killer. Naturally, this became my next 'hang-up', which was not shed until ten years later when I was commanding a squadron in Iraq. My enjoyment of this unexpected command was spoiled by the 'consumption' eating away at my lungs, month in and month out. I lost weight, could not sleep and prepared to die.

I had seen a film in which Chopin coughed his way through a concerto, splattering his crisp white cuffs with dark spots until, in a crescendo of music and a bloody efflux, he ended his life in a crimson pool on the ivory keys. In my case it was a somewhat less spectacular event. I was cleaning my teeth when I noticed the blood. After weeks of worry this was the only evidence I needed to confirm my self-diagnosis. It was important now to arrange my return home and say a fond farewell to my parents. There was no choice but to go to the hospital; they would fix the flight home.

I told the doctor that I was suffering from the terminal stages of consumption and invited him to confirm my findings by using his stethoscope. This was not unlike the one, casually hung up on the door, which in company with a huge grandfather clock had kept me awake as a child in my sister's Edinburgh house, haunting me with dark thoughts of time and death. He declined and asked me very gently instead what I was doing. He convinced himself that I was over-worked and, more importantly, convinced me that all I had was gum disease.

The reader will now understand that from a very early age I was a hypochondriac of the worst kind, too frightened to confirm his worst suspicions with the doctor. I have always been deeply ashamed of this weakness which has, pardon the pun, plagued my life. I have some excuse for it. My parents were old and my father's Parkinson's Disease cast a long shadow over my early life. I have learned that many others, especially men, suffer similar mental torments. As a result I have tried to be sensitive to the fears of children and not to dismiss their cries of help for relief from a worse agony than blows.

The discourse above was necessary to enable the reader to understand my frame of mind on my return from that first overseas tour. Walking dreamlike through London, with suitcases in tow, I decided that what was needed more than anything was food. The bacon and eggs were still sizzling as the plate was put in front of me. I picked up my knife and fork and with this my hands promptly froze, rendering me unable to eat. At last Parkinson's had struck. Leaving my food paid for but untouched on the table, I made my way to my sister Biddy in Croydon.

I really cannot remember if I told her first about the recent tragic events or of my latest disease, but I do recall her pointing out that carrying two heavy suitcases for long periods of time tends to make your hands tremble. I had to agree, as I demolished the enormous meal she had put in front of me. For the time being anyway, my 'Parkinson's' was cured.

My first night out in Hastings was to the Church Hall. Far from being the sedate affair that church dances tended to be, I was confronted by a beat I had never heard before and was totally unimpressed by the gyrations going on around the floor which passed for dancing. Apparently it was called 'rock and roll'. I sat out the whole evening and was on the point of going home when I got into conversation with a Hungarian who had just escaped from the uprising. Our adventure back to Egypt had diverted attention from this cruel suppression. Could we have done anything to help? Should we have done anything? Would the world war we were so anxious to avoid have been precipitated?

The Air Ministry offered me a posting to Manby, which they implied was close to my home in South East England. I gratefully accepted and waited for the official posting notice to come through. Manby, near Grimoldby, Lincolnshire, told me why I had not been able to find Manby in the family Atlas. I was to take more care in future regarding such offers.

What can I say about Manby? It was a beautiful old Mess and I made a good friend in my civilian batman. His name was Collington but he was universally known as 'Colly'. A splendid watercolour artist, he painted pictures which looked like colour-photographs. He was quietly encouraging about my own efforts with oils. I once found a note attached to one. He had written that at 20 yards my work looked reasonable but at 200 it was a 'B' sight better!

My job demanded my presence on the 25-yard range on most days, where I managed to remain alive despite the efforts of the trainees to shoot me. Their favourite trick was to point a Sten gun at me and whilst playing with the cocking stud, tell me it was jammed. A more interesting aspect of the work was lecturing on the effects of nuclear war and how to mitigate them. This was a time of great danger. We were led to believe that the Americans and the Russians, and more latterly ourselves, had aircraft armed with atomic bombs airborne at all times with pre-selected targets. In the event of nuclear attack the aircraft would continue on and destroy their targets. If this was so, it was a frightening game of brinkmanship fraught with potential for disaster by accident or design.

I took this very seriously and built a model town called 'Boom City', in which I placed small radioactive sources. The students were required to use radiac monitoring instruments to measure the levels of radiation and build up an isodose map from the results of their findings. Despite all my attempts I could not get the enthusiasm of my fellow officers for this kind of training. It was left to the Commanding Officer, after complementing me on my efforts, to tell me that neither he, nor anyone else on the base 'could give a witch's tit about nuclear war'. If it happened we would be dead and that was that!

Hardly surprising that, professionally, I turned my mind to other things. I have mentioned elsewhere the plethora of secondary duties that came my way. Not only the riding stable and the delightful Miss Margaret but also command of the station guard of honour, responsibility for the theatre club, the station band and the shooting club. I took over and completely reorganised the unit fire and rescue services but, more than anything else, I flew everything I could fly.

16. On Secondary Duties

An old 'hairy' once told me that there was more to Secondary Duties than just 'a tick in the box'. He surely must have known about Margaret and Pat, the one a girl, the other a horse. Girls were my special interest then and it's true to say that, in my intellect, they rivalled horses for the position of supreme unfathomability.

Margaret was, on reflection, a shrewd, calculating and delicious witch who operated within the body of a petite creature with short blonde hair. This seemingly helpless denizen of the Station Riding Stable would never have used the indefinite article in that or any other title. She spoke something like this. "Aye, Station Stables were not far from Station Pig Farm tha' know – and if tha' use tha' nose tha'd know". The Pig Farm, incidentally, was the alternative 'very rewarding secondary duty' offered by the Adjutant, in those days a great power in the land, before whom all did homage. Neither did I know then that the Commanding Officer's Secretary used to visit this homage on 'The Adj' at that unlikely venue.

To be scrupulously honest, when I made the decision I was unaware that the fair Margaret existed, but rejected pigs outright, having once been chased by a man-eating porker, or perhaps a small-boy-eating porker. A nice difference, which was no more apposite at the time than it is to this episode, but I will beg leave to return to it, if I ever describe 'escapades on the prison farm' or 'my family, Hitler and other boyhood chums'.

The sight of little Margaret, pitchfork in hand, 'mucking out', convinced me that my choice was the right one. The smell of hay, the freckled face, the blue eyes, the button nose, the warm and pleasant proportions garbed in breeches and shirt, the rapt attention, gave promise of delights untold. I knew that Paradise was within my grasp but three obstacles stood in my way. Firstly, an officer does not fraternise with employees. Secondly, the place was swarming with little girls, all of whom loved Margaret and some of whom saw romance in the air and did their level best to promote it, encouraged, I have to say, by their mothers! But it was the horses, which I have never credited with a lot of sense, horse or otherwise, and in particular 'Lady Pat' which combined to bring about my undoing.

It was the day after Margaret and I had submerged in my old Wolsey Wasp, one of several cars of distinction, personality, not to mention wire wool and sticky paste that have punctuated my travelling career, a ford (that is a watery crossing rather than a model T or something) had leapt into my car through the loosest floorboard and the ensuing fountain had stopped the car dead in its tracks and soaked us both to the skin.

Margaret's father, she graphically reported, was not a man to be trifled with. He was very large, had a very red face and was a bastion of the local farming community. That I was not a member of 'The Young Farmers', or better still a 'Landed Gent', would of itself have been sufficient grounds for my expulsion; but "A Raff Officer" (as he pronounced it) seemed totally reasonable grounds for summary execution.

Anyway, it was the day after this minor setback that saw the start of the 'Lady Pat Affair'. She had always been a gentle and kindly creature, the children's favourite. Nobody knew just how long she had been at the stable but all agreed it was many years. She chose this day to start on her journey to a better world, but one in which she could have been no better loved.

These lofty thoughts were far from my mind when Margaret told me, "Old Lady Pat's got staggers." Horses, no matter how kind, are very heavy and tend to squash small people. The Vet was called and his decision was sudden and chilling. "She's got to be put down for 'er sake and fer t'kids". Now putting down horses was strictly new territory for me. I could see that turning her loose was not an option but it was the manner of her disposal, rather than the means of her despatch, that was to haunt my every waking moment for a week.

"Knackers yard will give thee a tenner fer carcass," seemed like worthwhile advice to someone with my simple grasp of economics. In the recent past, a colourful trip to buy horses at Leicester had put me wise to the guile of pretty horse breeders and their tweed-suited mothers, at some expense to the fund that I ran. Not to mention considerable embarrassment in having to explain a highly improbable story to a remarkably patient and tolerant Station Commander, a leader whose compassion was only exhausted when he heard his adjutant answer the phone with the words "Hello, Station Pig Farm, duty pig squeaking!"

I looked through my window at the commotion outside in the road. This was the 1950s. It felt modern enough at the time but 'modern' did not include placards and street demos; not, that is, in Britain; not, that is, on an RAF Station; not, that was, until the case of Lady Pat.

'Don't Murder Pat'. 'Hands off Pat'. The banners screamed at me as the children, subdued but all the more sinister for that, walked by, accompanied by the same mothers who but a short time ago had been so anxious to marry me off. The telephone bell was a welcome distraction but short-lived enough. "Mrs Streams here," I recognised at once the voice of the wife of a resident Air Officer. "Peter, tell me it isn't true. You are not really going to send Pat to the Knackers Yard? The children will be horrified, the parents mortified and civilisation as we know it will pass away..."

Or words to that effect.

I felt numb. How had the children found out? Only Margaret could have told them. Surely not! Could her father have cooked up this conspiracy? Even more unlikely, what about Lady Pat? One or two more imaginative children claimed she could speak. Whatever the truth of it 'the cat was out of the bag' or 'the horse was out of its stable' and somehow fate had cast me in the role of executioner. I didn't flinch when I told Margaret and the gently sobbing children that Lady Pat was cremated because the same disease that had caused her sickness had saved her from the cook pot. But as I scattered the ashes from a billet stove over the fresh green pasture, I could not help being consumed with curiosity as to who got the tenner.

17. Ill Met in Grimsby

At that time an RAF station in rural Lincolnshire was a closed community, like village life in an eighteenth century novel. The Officer's Mess was the big house and the hive of social activity. Those of us living in the Mess were treated like landed gentry and waited on hand and foot. The food was local, gamey and magnificent. At weekends breakfasts ran till lunch, followed by tea, with dinner at seven. There was always a little cheese, biscuits and chutney left out for supper should it be needed. Ladies might visit the Mess but could only be entertained in the Ladies Room or the Music Room. At weekends and in the evenings, older children were allowed to accompany their parents to the bar and it was there that many romances between young officers and eligible daughters flourished.

The wives' club, the flower club, highland dancing clubs, societies, dramatic and music flourished and within them gossip and tittle-tattle abounded and was the very stuff of life. I do believe that each unmarried officer had a dossier on them in which their attributes, foibles and failures were duly noted. Escape was difficult. The town of Louth, never lively except on market days, seemed to close altogether at weekends. The bells of the ancient church, one of which was cracked, day and night tolled the quarters and the hours with discordant predictability. Then there was the seaside, seasonal hurly-burly of Skegness and the quiet of Mablethorpe and beyond that the Mecca of the fishing industry – Grimsby.

She was a black-haired beauty and she was discrete. Indeed, discretion from the outset of the short-lived romance was of the essence, not the least because she was the personal typist for the Station Commander, the very epicentre of the local Service community and in the Mess, a mighty Zeus in a temple of minor gods. More importantly, her name had been linked by the gossips with that of the Adjutant, a power in the land.

On the night that they had plotted and schemed to be together the young man was well prepared for any outcome, care of the camp barber who, needless to say, operated from within the Mess. Not that he could place much trust in him because barbers are talkers. Nevertheless, the purchases were made with considerable Catholic soul searching and acute embarrassment, then tucked away in the breast coat pocket behind a folded handkerchief, just in case...

They chose a delightful hotel far off the beaten track for their assignation. No one would find them there. They enjoyed a fine meal and a little wine. Things were going extraordinarily well and the night was full of promise.

"Will you take coffee in the lounge?" the waiter asked.

Whilst the young man readily agreed, he knew that this might make them more vulnerable to discovery but hesitation at this juncture might set back his chances of success.

The girl from the typing pool looked at the young man's partner with ill-disguised surprise as the waiter led the couple to her table. This was restrained in comparison to the reaction of her escort, whose face was contorted with emotion.

"Er... Good Evening, old boy," said the adjutant, as he struggled to regain his composure.

The young man's partner blushed and in that moment looked more desirable than ever, but he knew then that it was all slipping away from him.

It seemed sensible to sit down and pretend to be nonchalant, the round mahogany table staring up at him as his mind protested the unfairness of it all.

"Will you have a drink?" said the adjutant, endeavouring to break the ice.

"It's so hot in here," the young man said, already trying to build for a skilful exit, who knows, something might yet be salvaged from this Grimsby wreck.

To emphasise the point he pulled out his carefully folded pocket hankie to mop his fevered brow...

All three hit the table at the same time!

18. The Great Fire of Manby

Ramtha was not to be my last experience of fire. The 'Great Fire of Manby' started in the long line of small workshops, offices and restrooms that ran the length of the standard aircraft hangars of the mid-thirties which straddled this old airfield on the flat lands of Lincolnshire. No doubt it had been smouldering for hours before an airman who, taken short, had happened to look out from a toilet window in the early hours of a cold winter's morning.

The man quickly alerted the telephone exchange who had a list of those who should be notified in case of fire. Top of the list was an Air Marshal, followed by his deputy, followed by an Air Commodore, followed by his deputy, followed by the Station Commander, followed by the Duty Officer, followed by the Orderly Officer, followed by the Fire Officer, followed by the Fire Section and so on. The reader might be excused for imagining that by now the fire could happily be out or, more likely, out of control.

The Station Commander was first to react. His overcoat over his pyjamas and wearing his bedroom slippers, he leapt onto a bicycle and was hammering on the front door of the Fire Section as the call finally came through. Getting no immediate response, he flung down his bike and ran to the back of the building through which an airman was being despatched to the motor transport pool to bring the 'back up' vehicle. From this point things began to go awry...

The big red fire engine had always appealed to the 'old man', being similar, no doubt, to one his nanny had bought him sometime before he became a highly-decorated wartime pilot, so the Fire Chief's invitation to climb aboard did not have to be made twice. He stood proudly at the front of the machine as, with bells ringing and lights flashing, it leapt out of the space left as the automatic doors opened. He may not have been the first to see his bicycle before it was mounted by the machine, which quickly came to rest atop the mangled remains, but he was certainly the first to answer the inevitable question.

"What dozy c*** has left his f***ing bicycle there?"

Never mind, our other man is now hot footing it down to the Motor Transport Section to recover the second fire engine, which is on a trickle charge to protect it from the vagaries of the damp Lincolnshire air and to ensure that it is always ready to pounce. He feverishly opens the side gate with his special key. Now he is aboard the vehicle and the Alvis engine starts on the button. The main gates loom up and he stops abruptly. They are locked for security!

He switches off, jumps down, runs back through the little gate and gallops back to the guardroom. This is the Mecca of all security and holds all the keys in duplicate and twice. On the way he meets some of the fire team from the disabled vehicle running to join him.

"All right, all right," says the duty policeman, who is even lower on the wretched list of people to be informed. "Where's the bleedin' fire?"

Whilst the professionals did their very worst, the gallant little airman who had originally reported the conflagration was quickly mustering the troops to tackle the blaze by themselves. They opened the hangar doors and wheeled out several large aircraft which were full of fuel, but their fire-fighting efforts were less commendable. They knew how to run out hose reels but did not know how to link up with the hydrants. They picked up and threw away as useless, fire extinguishers, which needed only to be turned upside down to work, although I never quite believed the story that one man succeeded in following the instructions printed on the extinguishers by standing on his head. At last the Louth Fire Brigade arrived and the main hangar was saved.

The Officers' Mess was extraordinarily quiet the following morning as I wolfed down my bacon and eggs. By way of conversation and quite unaware of the events of the night, I mentioned to a friend who joined me that this was the day I was to become the Station Fire Officer. As the designate, I was not on the list at all and it took him, and several others, some time to convince me of what had taken place. I think the president of the board of inquiry had his doubts too.

The alerting list was changed that night. With hindsight it seemed like a good idea to call the Fire Section first when fire broke out. The week-long training I endured to make me an expert, or maybe 'ex-spurt' was interesting. Leaping off a 100-foot tower and escaping from a burning aircraft was exciting but my tour of duty as a fire officer was uneventful. After all, lightning seldom strikes twice in the same place, especially if you are ready for it.

I was reminded of these events some years later when lightning struck just the once! No longer a fire officer, I watched with interest as the officers' mess at Akrotiri was burned to the ground. The sweating, smoke-bedraggled figure of the Station Commander could be seen trying to direct the operations of the local fire brigade. The station fire section was late to arrive. I really did not care to ask who had been told first, or enquire after the health of the station commander's bike. Perhaps because I was reeling with disgust that the only thing to be saved, at some risk to the rescuer, was the ledger containing all our mess bills!

"Brave misguided fool," said some.

"Creep!" said others.

"*Plus ça change...*" said I.

19. Goodbye Old Soldier

I had spent the weekend in London and took my fiancée to visit Biddy and Ted and their children Margaret and John in Croydon. The long journey back to rural Lincolnshire that Sunday evening, nursing my ancient car, was cold, lonely and tiresome and I was relieved to see the spire of the old church at Louth appearing through the frosty March gloom.

The hall porter at the Officers Mess at Manby looked up from his newspaper.

"Glad I caught you sir," he said, "a Brigadier has been telephoning. You need to contact him urgently."

It only took me a moment to realise that this was Tony, husband of my sister Frances, who by use of his colourful imagination could always be relied on to grab people's attention.

"It's Dad," he said, in his chirpy Glaswegian accent. "He has had a stroke and is very ill. Can you come straight away?" Even a make-believe brigadier should have understood that junior officers cannot just leave their post and go, although, truth be told, his real army experience would have had him do just that, regardless of the consequences.

It took some time the following day to arrange a relief and some leave and re-embark on the long journey down south in my aching car. It was dark and foreboding when I arrived in Hastings and I made straight for the house to be greeted at the door by Tony. He barred my entrance and insisted on taking me for a 'stiff drink' to fortify me for the night ahead.

Tony reported, in fairly graphic terms, that my father was difficult for my mother to handle and had been almost violent with him. This latter piece of information was no great surprise because Dad had scant regard for Tony when in the best of health but as the last stages of Parkinson's disease wrought their havoc and as his speech failed, he mistook kind words for condescension and physical help as an assault.

It was going to be a difficult night but I had lived with Parkinson's since the age of twelve. I knew my sick father better than the well one, the one who had ruled the roost over brothers and sisters. I knew his moods and foibles, his frustration and his sense of entrapment in an ailing body but at that moment I was conscious of something else – resentment and impatience with him, which I had never felt before.

This came to the fore when, a little while later, with Tony gone and my mother asleep, he and I sat alone in the front room of the little house that had been our home for ten years. I had just reassured him that the spots he saw on everything he looked at were a symptom of his condition when he started to complain of something else. I rounded on him, reminded him that despite the gap in our ages, we had much in common, not the least our journeys in Iraq – or Mesopotamia as it was in his day. Why had we not talked about that?

So began a night of feverish reminiscing, which only ended with the dawn. Much of what he said I have forgotten, besides which, stories of Ireland and India, of the police and prison service were well known to my family if not to me, but 'Mespot' was ours. I reminded him that Habbaniya was my base from which, as an Officer in the RAF Regiment which commanded the Iraq levies and provided ground forces, I had made many forays into the desert, east to Bagdad and west towards Jerusalem, north to Kirkuk and south to the airfield at Shiba and the nearby fabled port of Basra.

"I was with Maude in Bagdad," he said. Thinking he was referring to my mother, who he always called 'Maud', and anxious that he remained sensible, I chided him with his foolishness. He laughed, for the first time since my arrival. "It was..." he stammered out, "...it was General Maude, you daft bugger!"

Habbaniya was so called because it was close to a lake of the same name. It is close to the Euphrates and is served by a 'cut' or canal, which irrigates the area and turns desert into verdant green. In describing its location to my father, I mentioned that it was between two towns. One was called Fallujah and the other Ramadi. It was at Ramadi that he witnessed the horrors of war on a massive scale, served with distinction and was commissioned in the field.

The terror of it all remained with him throughout his life and now invaded our last night together.

In the morning my mother came in to tell me that my one hour shift was over and now it was her turn. I doubt she ever knew that, after so many disturbed nights, she had slept for nine hours! The Doctor came a little later and decisions had to be made. My mother could no longer look after him. He was a big man and she was less than five feet high. When he was coherent it had been hard work but now, following a cerebral haemorrhage, he was irascible and difficult to fathom. I could stay a few days but not for ever.

The doctor was in no doubt that Dad should go into a nursing home, if only for a few days so that my mother could recover her strength. I think he knew that a further stroke was on the cards anyway. There was, as always, a question of expense, but most of all there was my father's objection to leaving his home. It was left to me to make the decision. I made the wrong one and it will always haunt me.

I followed the ambulance to the home and saw him in. His last words to me were "You've let me down." A sad memory which I cannot expunge. He died the following day, after a 'disturbed' night. I should have been with him.

Fortunately my brothers and the rest of the family were now on hand to take over the 'arrangements'. He was buried in Hastings cemetery and Alby, Paul and I were all in uniform to salute and say our farewells. The date was the 9th of March 1959. I was just twenty-four and had lost my Dad, his last words ringing in my ears.

Soon, with me engaged on flying training, our little home was sold and my link with childhood was gone.

20. 'Echo Foxtrot Rolling!'

Now flying at Manby as a hobby almost eight years after I first took to the air was something different. It was for pleasure and it was varied; an Anson this week, a Meteor next, then a flight in a Lincoln and finally the piston (propeller driven) Provost. The Lincoln was undoubtedly the most exciting as we made our way from Manby to Ballykelly in Northern Ireland. I was positioned in the bomb aimer's place, face down on a large perspex window. The ground below was a moving tapestry of fields, woodlands, lakes and rivers. Then, from my magic carpet, the grey/blue of the Irish Sea, choppy in the morning sunlight.

I flew at every opportunity, but it was the Provost in which most of my 'hands-on' experience was obtained. Indeed, my skills developed well beyond the point at which I should normally have flown solo. Those who flew with me were convinced that I should ask, once again, to fly for a living. Maybe I should not have listened. Maybe the opportunity to fly at the grand old age of twenty six should not have been extended to me, but when it was, I rejoiced in it.

Syerston was a large training airfield on the Fosse Way, close to Newark in Nottinghamshire. The Fosse Way is a long, straight Roman road which, from the air, points to an airfield called Wymeswold, where we used to practice take-offs and landings. I say points, because just a few minutes flying time away from that destination it dog-legs away towards Leicester. Those Romans clearly had it in for me because whilst the journey out was easy, the problems of picking up the road to fly back after forty minutes of 'circuits and bumps' posed a threat which was almost to be my downfall.

It was a joyous day when my instructor, showing a woeful absence of judgement and considerable professional courage, climbed out of the aircraft and said, "It's all yours." All mine. How long had I waited for this moment? Yet now it had come it was something of an anti-climax. The Jet Provost was, to my mind, quite unlike its piston stablemate. Most people would have welcomed its smooth and regular acceleration and the rapid response of the controls. Everyone said that it was a very forgiving aircraft and no doubt everyone was right. But I did not like it at all. The piston Provost had engine torque, the controls were heavy, the throttle roared, you had to wrestle with it a bit, but it was a live thing under your seat. Not so the Jet Provost. To me it was a smooth, quiet but soulless space capsule.

Now these are fanciful thoughts which would be derided by experienced aviators but that's the way I felt, and in this frame of mind I set off one fateful day to fly solo to Wymeswold, care of my Roman navigation. I see now the bend in the road, I swallow hard and keep straight ahead. Suddenly, I see it there in front and below, its runways and perimeter track wet and black but no less welcoming for that. "Echo Foxtrot joining from Syerston," my voice a practised calm. The tower gave me wind speed and direction over the live runway, together with the barometric pressure to adjust my altimeter. All set for the first landing.

The landing was perfect and after some thirty minutes of circuits and bumps my only task now was to take on some fuel and return. I walked away from the aircraft during the refuelling and dug deep into my flying overalls for my pipe, tobacco and matches. The pipe was a fairly recent acquisition to my image and in some respects a source of considerable irritation. Whether tightly packed with borrowed tobacco, or lightly filled with my own, it seemed a very difficult beast to keep alight. So it proved on this day until I finally gave up in exasperation and stuffed it back in my pocket.

All the while, the Roman gods were watching, biding their time, poised to strike.

"Echo Foxtrot, airborne for Syerston," my clipped advice to the tower giving no hint of my pleasure at yet another smooth take off. I eased back the throttle and managed to suppress the nagging worry about navigating my return. For the first time in days I felt a warm feeling of achievement surging over me. It was also at this moment, as the aircraft hurtled down the runway and shook the ground from its wheels, that I realised the warm feeling was not entirely an inner glow.

My pocket was smouldering; it was the damned pipe, perverse as usual. Airborne at two hundred feet, I was on fire. Should I tell the tower? Perhaps a calm "Echo Foxtrot I am on fire" would do the trick. This would have produced a series of questions and instructions about engine fire warning lights, jet pipe temperatures, extinguishers and preparations to eject. All to be curtailed by an admission that it was *me* that was on fire and not the wretched aircraft! Ejecting or putting out the engine would not help me at all. I decided not to tell and beat my overalls furiously in the hope that I could extinguish it.

It seemed to have worked but now, able once again to concentrate on flying the aircraft, I noticed that my undercarriage was still down. I selected the button marked 'Undercarriage up'. There was no reaction. Then, 'Undercarriage down'. Still no joy. I repeated the performance time and again but all my frenetic button pushing was to no avail; the wheels remained firmly down. Still very low and very fast, I eased back the control column to gain height and lose speed and as I did, a reassuring clunk told me that my undercarriage was up.

I began to regain my composure. It seemed that the fire was out and the wheels were up; time now to look outside and navigate home. Shock, horror! A large city was sprawled out beneath me. My mind was doing cartwheels. How long had I spent firefighting and tinkering with the undercarriage? If I had flown in a straight line, then a 180 degree turn would take me back to Wymeswold. But, sadly, by the time this simple expedient occurred to me I had already ducked and weaved in the hope of seeing the Roman road. I was lost!

By now I was flying over the centre of the city and my guess that it was Leicester coincided with the discovery, prompted by the close proximity of the buildings, that I was reading my altimeter wrongly and flying dangerously low.

"Get a grip," I heard myself say. I climbed to altitude and headed in the general direction of Syerston. When I saw the city outskirts give way to country I plucked up courage and used my radio.

"Echo Foxtrot, request check steer." I used this message because it could have meant that I knew my position but just wanted confirmation. The Tower responded immediately and their questions left me in no doubt that they were not fooled.

They gave me instructions to climb even further and follow a heading at about 90 degrees from the direction I was going. At last, there were the familiar shapes of the huge cooling towers close to Newark. The airfield came in sight.

"Echo Foxtrot joining," my voice sang out confidently. They could not see me at first because they were looking for me at 1200 feet, the circuit height. Once again I had allowed the aircraft to descend and, as I thrust forward the throttle and climbed, I noticed the tops of the grid pylons at barely more than shoulder height.

"We have you," came a relieved voice from the tower and, as the landing instructions were passed, I saw the array of fire tenders and ambulances, obviously for some kind of emergency. It did not occur to me that I was it. The runway loomed up in front; offering a chance to demonstrate my new found skill with a smooth landing. It was not to be. The aircraft hit the ground and bounced. Several times. Oblivious of my now very low fuel state, I convinced myself that I must go round again and get it right. The entire tower must have groaned as they saw me accelerate down the runway and heard me call, "Echo Foxtrot, Rolling..."

A very determined voice put me in no doubt that as I came round for my next landing, I was to stick!

I had enough fuel left to taxi to dispersal ... just!

It must have been a week or so after this escapade, in clear sky and within sight of the airfield – just in case – that I undertook a stimulating solo aerobatics exercise: spinning and recovering, inverse flight ... the lot. I was an 'ace'. The return and landing was uneventful but as I sat in the crew room afterwards, spots began to appear before my eyes. They got bigger and bigger until, almost blind, I asked someone to take me to the medical centre. The doctor had just left for lunch and nobody, not even me, thought this an emergency.

The minutes ticked by and with them speckled vision gradually returned, the spots getting smaller and smaller until, with the lunch hour almost up, my full sight was returned. 'No need to see the doctor now,' I thought, and made a swift exit before he came back. What a silly man. I could now add the fear of sudden blindness to my list of anxieties. I could envisage another long cross-country navigational exercise like the one I had recently undertaken, with the constant prospect of going blind. Imagination in a mind where the defences are down through lack of sleep can engulf and destroy.

It all happened very quickly at the end. Tired out by late nights of catching up on 'ground studies' and with my instructor away on leave, I was asked to fly with my squadron commander. He was as unimpressed with my performance as I was with him. The chief instructor, his face a worthy testament to the skills of the plastic surgeon, flew with me next and tested me out on my 'orientation'. After a little while he asked me where we were in relation to the airfield, or even the world! I forget the details but he had me by my Achilles' heel and the end result was 'the chop'. An honourable chop but the chop nevertheless.

"We have been very impressed with your officer-like qualities and want you to stay in the RAF. So what would you like to do?"

"I will be a navigator," I replied, to a howl of laughter from the Suspension Board.

Years later, I stood before a scar-faced air marshal who was to decide if I should have a regular commission.

"Did you do flying training?" he asked. Detecting my hesitation, he looked up from his papers and recognition dawned. "You were the silly bugger who wanted to be a navigator," he said.

Clearly, I had made my mark.

21. Salute... He Moves!

The Equipment Officers at Manby were amongst my closest friends and from the outset I held the view, rather like Napoleon, that if all other things are equal in war, the battle goes to the best quartermaster. So, when they asked me what I would like to do apart from fly or return to the Regiment with my tail between my legs, I found myself volunteering to join the ranks of the quartermasters.

A few weeks of Equipment Training convinced me that I had made a terrible mistake. To have to track the seemingly interminable progress of a stores voucher through an Equipment Supply Depot, forecast the consumption of split pins or produce accounting records for a miscellany of almost valueless items was indescribably boring. It was also largely unnecessary, despite the overworked line about a kingdom being lost for the sake of a nail. Indeed, in those early days I felt that I was amongst accountants rather than pragmatists; people quick to see the reasons for not doing things, slaves of the written procedure, small-minded, petty folk with whom I had nothing in common.

I was, in fact, part of an officer course of rejects of one sort or another, rumoured to be the worst in living memory. Our sins included raiding the Sergeants Mess and leaving in an intoxicated condition, attempting to burn down the Officers Mess and standing up the Commanding Officer's daughter. As one intimately concerned with all three events listed, I can say with some certainty that our transgressions were somewhat exaggerated, but when the Commanding Officer said that he was beside himself with rage at our collective behaviour and I broke into a then popular song entitled 'I'm Walking Beside You', he became as convinced as his chief instructor that I was not a son of the Equipment Branch.

The chief instructor was a Scot with a long, drooping moustache who bore an uncanny resemblance to his dog, which I named 'Shoop'. It was a kind of longhaired sheepdog, more sheep than dog, and suffered from acute melancholia. It was not long before dog and master were identified by the same title. They dragged themselves from lecture to lecture and wallowed in the boredom of it all. He quickly recognised my flippancy and/or resistance to brain-washing and did his best to help me on my path to self-destruction.

The last modules on the course were to do with 'Fuels' and 'Movements'. Although I never quite mastered the intricacies of the aircraft trim sheet, my results were of such a high order that, to the disgust of the directing staff, the overall pass mark for the course was achieved. They were further bewildered when the Air Ministry posted me as Senior Equipment Officer to a small station in Essex called Chigwell, the home of a Ground Radio Servicing Unit of Signals Command.

My right-hand man was a Warrant Officer who did all the de-tailed work and allowed me to develop ideas and chase girls. He also almost taught me to play golf.

Then there was Kerstin.

22. Kerstin's English Usage

She still says 'peanuts' in the most provocative way and from time to time there are other lapses but otherwise her English is fluent. It was not always thus. When I first asked her to dance in that 'den of iniquity', the Hastings Pier and did my first foxtrot to a quickstep, I had no idea that she was a foreigner. The dance number finished almost before it began and it was as I tried to invite her to dance yet another foxtrot, this time to a slow waltz, that I understood that she could speak little English and she understood that I could only dance the foxtrot! She was pretty in an elfin kind of way and, perhaps because she seemed so vulnerable, I kissed her gently on the forehead.

We remained together for the rest of the evening. She hesitated to accept a ride in my 1935 Wolsey Wasp, not for fear of me, but that the car might not have a test certificate! We arranged to meet the following day. As we kissed goodnight she said her first comprehensible English, which was "Hello, Goodbye, Jolly Good, 2 o'clock on the pier". 'Hey' in Swedish means both 'hello' and 'goodbye'.

Strangely enough, the first language howler was not of her doing, but my own. It was the Hastings Corporation 'Flathat' on duty at the gate of Hastings castle who caused it.

"Sorry Guv, gates close at five." I should add that it was one minute past five at the time. Kerstin only said a couple of words to convince the poor man that we were both aliens. 'Flathat' put his bespectacled nose as close to mine as he could and said in a very loud voice. "ALL CLOSED NOW. NOT OPEN. MUST GO FOR MY TEA," at which he made exaggerated tea-drinking movements, accompanied by loud slurping noises.

My instinct was to say "Well go and have your tea, you silly arse," but discretion got the better of me and I said in my best Scandinavian sing-song, "So we will come tomorrow."

Honour was satisfied.

Come to think of it, the next memorable communication difficulty was also not of her making. My mother was convinced that all Swedes were 'lapsed' (she meant Laps) or Eskimos. "They all sit on big skins in the middle of dung huts with a fire in the centre and a hole in the roof." All my efforts to convince her that Sweden was technically much more advanced than Britain were to no avail.

My mother was taken aback when she saw this pretty girl in her little blue dress and completely bowled over when Kerstin curtsied and offered her hand. She got the best cups and silver teapot treatment and everything was going well until mother started asking about the Swedish houses.

"You must be very cold in the winter," she said, imagining the mud huts with the hole in the roof now covered in snow and looking for all the world like igloos. Kerstin could well understand why anyone living in draughty British homes with no double, never mind triple glazing, should think that way. Searching to find the words to describe central heating she said, "We have a fire in the centre of the house which makes us all very warm."

"Told you so!" said my mother.

Days later I gave Kerstin a redundant engagement ring, whereupon she announced with great solemnity that we were now 'engined'. It was some time before the meaning and impact of her assumption struck me, by which time I quite liked the idea of being 'engined'. Nevertheless, for the time being and for the first few weeks of our marriage, the dictionary was to be our constant companion.

Mrs Law was our next door neighbour and a real salt of the earth cockney lady with an acquiescent husband. To say she was fat would be a gross, so to speak, understatement. She took to Kerstin straight away. They went shopping together and she explained the various cuts of meat and named the hundred and one things needed in the kitchen and the home, which were called altogether different names from those in Sweden.

Mrs Law decided that she would cook a meat pudding for us. Mr Law duly delivered it to the door. As he left, Kerstin said, with tremendous feeling, "Kindest regards to the Pudding".

The gales of laughter we heard through the paper-thin walls of our 'semi' that followed his return were evidence enough that the message had been passed on in full.

23. No Stayin' Power

Whether it was because I was to be a Movements Officer, or because Kerstin was pregnant, or because it was my birthday, I cannot say with any degree of certainty, but we were to go to Cyprus by sea. The troopship that was to be our home for ten days was the SS *Nevasa*, a large, single-funnelled vessel of the British India Line. We were to sail on 7th March – my birthday.

Kerstin was very protective of her unborn baby and almost from the outset used to pat her stomach, making soothing noises whilst talking gentle gibberish. Only that unfathomable look of fulfilment in her eyes showed me that she was even 'with child'. To her, the child was already an individual in her care, a friend, travelling companion and purpose for living. I am not sure I quite understood then, or now. Does any man?

Whatever tender thoughts I had for my child or wife, my purpose for living, it seemed, was to be in charge of the Royal Air Force party of men embarked on the ship. After settling Kerstin in a rather splendid double cabin I made my way to see the Ship's Commandant. I should explain that whilst the captain sailed the ship, the Commandant ordered the lives of the huge contingent of troops, in this case two thousand men of the Gloster Regiment. These were the 'Glorious' Glosters' famed for their action in the Napoleonic Wars and more recently in Korea at the battle of the Imgin River. Just fifty young and spotty RAF cooks and clerks provided the glorious RAF contribution to this gallant company.

I entered the Commandant's cabin in response to a curt "Come!" to my knock. He was in 'blues' and sat behind a large oak desk. My salute prompted a brief smile and a broad wink, all of which rested uneasily on his sallow, careworn and lined face. As I returned the wink with a nod and a grin, his face changed into a grimace, followed by a twitch and another wink, all reinforced by a short grunt. The man's face was mobile and I soon lost the battle to keep up with the kaleidoscope of changing emotions writ large on his shell-shocked face. Worse, I had somehow to unscramble the mess I had got myself into by my casual and friendly greeting.

The dilemma was short-lived because he launched into a torrent of words about deck games, competitions, and the like, which he thought I should organise between my fifty 'erks' and the entire Gloster Regiment. At least in this respect it was fortunate that the weather took a hand. The good ship *Nevasa* was barely out of the sound of the brass band playing 'Auld Lang Syne' before we were in the teeth of a Channel gale. Monstrous seas crashed over the bows and the decks heaved. So began a voyage in which we were to be hit by successive storms, punctuated only by fuelling stops at Gibraltar and Malta.

For Kerstin, in early pregnancy, seasickness compounded her plight. Mornings began with the same words every day from our Indian steward. "Wedder no bloody good". Indeed, it soon became clear that his entire gift of English was 'bloody good' or 'no bloody good' with the odd noun thrown in. Miserable day followed miserable night for Kerstin who, between bouts of sickness, patted her tummy and worried about the 'poor little chap'. In contrast, I dressed for dinner every night and shared the dining room with the captain, ship's officers and a dwindling number of other passengers.

The first respite from the weather came as we sailed into Gibraltar and came under the lee of the land. The sun shone and Kerstin, drawn by the prospect of firm ground, was dressed and ashore with me in the first party. We left Gibraltar that same evening and watched until the great fortress rock was lost in the gathering gloom on a red horizon. The following day was windy but fine. This was to be the day of the great contest.

Battle lines were soon drawn up, the Glosters on one side, the Royal Air Force on the other, a heavy rope between us. The Glosters had a 'barker' or team leader in the shape of an enormous Pioneer Corps Staff Sergeant, who sported a heavy ginger beard and moustache and, for reasons which still escape me, carried a pickaxe helve.[1] The RAF team was encouraged – 'led' seems altogether too

---

[1] Handle.

strong a word for it – by a weedy little corporal who, as it turned out, made up in ingenuity what he lacked in other quarters.

The rope extended from almost one side of the ship to the other and I noticed a knot of people around the RAF end. What I did not see at the time was another knot connecting the rope to a nylon cord, which, at its other extremity, was firmly affixed to the taffrail.[2] The supporters were so well positioned that none of this was visible from the Gloster camp or from the upper deck, where stood spectators, the Commandant and me.

"Take the strain!" boomed Ginger of the Glosters.

"Hold on lads," squeaked his opposite number.

The rope grew taut. Ginger worked himself up into a frenzy, getting ready to give the executive word of command that would prove the opposition as feeble as it certainly looked. He worked his pickaxe helve up and down and finally, in a red-faced explosion, screamed "Heave!"

Nothing happened.

"HEAVE!" he repeated, his eyeballs standing out like toadstools from the ginger fungus.

The rope remained taut and the white hankie in the middle moved not one inch.

Ginger became apoplectic with rage and took to jumping up and down to add further weight to his exhortations. I have often pondered since what might have happened had the Glosters been strong enough. The rope might have parted, the taffrail might have been torn off, or perhaps the ship might have been pulled over. In the event, with Ginger almost hoarse from his vocals and his team exhausted by repeated attempts to capsize the ship, the RAF corporal, now grown in stature by his quiet presence and the rocklike steadiness of his team, said "Pull".

The hankie came over the line and the round was ours.

Ginger looked on, a broken man.

A good story might end on that happy note but life is not like that, is it? The Commandant glowered at me, his face working

---

[2] The aftermost railing around the stern of a ship, often, but not always, ornately carved.

overtime. "It's not over yet," he said. He showed none of the qualities of impartiality that I would have expected. Perhaps he was at the Imgin River too. Anyway, he was of course right, the rules of 'Tug of War' require the best of three pulls, so the teams duly changed ends, the reluctance of the RAF supporters to move away disguising frantic efforts to untie and conceal the nylon cord.

Alas, there was no opportunity to tie the cord to the other end of the rope. Ginger, after engaging in a quiet briefing of his team, which must have been heard from one end of the ship to the other, urged them to take the strain. Even this effort all but toppled the RAF team.

"Wait for it..." said Ginger, his confidence still dented by the outcome of the previous bout. "Puuuull!" he intoned, in a long subdued growl. The hankie moved their way and the tiebreaker was on us.

Ginger's confidence was completely restored. He clearly thought that this time all that was needed was a sudden pull and, no sooner than his troops were in position, he screamed the order. There was no doubt what he intended to do. He was going to pull that hankie and the hated enemy across the line. This was his Imgin. This was the Gloster Regiment. Fortunately, the RAF let go before being whiplashed into oblivion and the Glosters ran backwards, at an extraordinary speed, to finish in a pile at the side of the ship. Luckily no one was lost overboard. Ginger, his honour vindicated, jumped up and down and waved his helve in the air. The Commandant looked down his nose and said, "Typical Air Force. No stayin' power."

Thankfully, this confrontation was enough to pacify the Commandant until we reached Malta.

Although I had stopped at the airfield at Luqa on earlier occasions, this was the first opportunity to look about the island. Kerstin and I took a ride in a gharry, resplendent with horse and driver, and made our way up to the vantage point from which we could look over Grand Harbour. Malta was a sandstone rock sprinkled with sandcastles and, not for the first time in my life, I felt the presence of history.

I imagined the hordes of Suleiman the Magnificent crowding into the harbours and inlets. I could see the Janissaries screaming their way into battle against the Knights of St John. I could picture the Grand Master and tactician De Valetta directing the defence; by his side, a solitary English knight, Oliver Starkey. The scene changed in my mind's eye to a more recent conflict. The anti-aircraft guns were pouring tracer into the sky, pausing only to allow one or other of the three Bristol Gladiators, 'Faith', 'Hope' or 'Charity' to join battle.

The sandstone was hot to the touch, even under that March sky, as we made our way back to the *Nevasa* and put to sea once more. I could never quite believe those stories of St Paul's shipwrecks until that voyage on *Nevasa*. The winds that lashed the ship for the next two days were filled, not with rain but with sand. At least this put paid to any further games, or wars, and I was left to plod the decks and do what I could to comfort my young wife.

The Commandant did not trouble me again until I joined the retinue on his last inspection, amidst much boot crunching, saluting, shouting and pace stick waving by a motley collection of followers, including the infamous 'Ginger', still resplendent with his pickaxe helve. My own men were fairly comfortably housed above the waterline and 'passed muster' as they say. As we progressed further and further down into the very bowels of the ship, I saw a number of Gloster families who were not so lucky. Not for them the joy of a porthole. In cramped cabins, with only artificial light and dependent on unreliable air conditioning, they seemed totally resigned to their plight. Could it be they were mesmerised by the stick waving?

Conditions during most of the journey for these unfortunates must have been appalling and I was saddened but hardly surprised to learn that a child had died during the recent storm. Perhaps it was this that made me think it worse than it really was.

Kerstin no doubt thought that when you feel as ill as she did, surroundings make very little difference anyway, but by comparison with these people, we were living in unbridled luxury. It was nevertheless with considerable relief that we stepped ashore at Limassol the following day, Kerstin, 'the little chap' and me.

24. Nicosia

When I look back to Cyprus days I tend to forget that we spent some four months in Nicosia. During this time I was introduced to 'Movements' and we had our first child. The Air Movements organisation was very strange. The element that I worked for was to do with loading and unloading transport aircraft with passengers and cargo. It was fronted up by 'Fred', a Flight Lieutenant like me, except much older and with only one eye, like a character from a pirate ship, minus parrot. He and his wife were a highly sociable couple both inside and outside the RAF community.

Fred enjoyed the title of 'Senior Air Movements Officer' or 'SA-MO' for short. SAMO was responsible to a squadron leader, who also looked after a booking office that called forward cargoes and passengers to aircraft. One of the services offered to passengers and crew was currency exchange and the custom was to put all the new officers on to this task. As all the other officers had done their stint and all were qualified Movements Officers, having attended a course at the RAF Movements School, I accepted without demure, despite the fact that I was their senior.

There followed two or three truly horrific months, during which time I was at everyone's beck and call during a 24 hours on / 24 hours off cycle. I was accommodated in a cage inside a room without air-conditioning; a sweatbox, with just enough room for me and my money. I had about £2,000 in various currencies which I had to add up and balance every few hours. I do not like closed, hot rooms and money frightens me. I never expected it to balance, so if it did I could not believe my luck and checked it again whereupon, needless to say, the result was invariably different. On many occasions I was out by more than a thousand pounds!

During one of these aberrations, towards the end of my stint, I was so convinced that I had made a dreadful mistake that I asked the squadron leader to double check my figures. They were correct but I think he got the message that I had had enough!

Shortly afterwards, Fred left and I became SAMO. There was much to be done because it seemed to me that the previous regime had left all the planning to the booking office until shortly before an aircraft landed or took off. I introduced folders, which started with the first intimation of a mission (a flight) and were not finished with until everything had been completed and the flight was history.

Then I set about painting the yard with the outlines and dimensions of the cargo holds of each aircraft type and actually loaded up the squares with the cargo appropriate to that compartment. In this way, aircraft loads could be pre-planned. Things started to go very well and I gained the respect of the other officers. Then the CO was posted and a new squadron leader arrived in a blaze of glory, determined to stamp his mark on the organisation. I don't think he liked me much – even before I nicknamed him 'Spartacus' – and when the opportunity came to get out from under and go to the bomber base at Akrotiri, I went.

But things had been going on in my private life as well. We lived at a place called the Agrottis Flats, close to one of the hotels used by the Movements Organisation to put up passengers and crews. The hotel proprietor and his wife, introduced to us by Fred, were instrumental in us getting into the flats, which were rather nice and new. They were extraordinarily kind, invited us to dinner and so on. New as I was to the world of business and commerce, I was never convinced that their kindness was without motive and I was probably wrong.

Several Army nursing sisters lived there, one of whom was a midwife. They were pleasant girls and it was reassuring to have them there. Kerstin had been really ill when we arrived; the sea voyage had knocked her out. She had kidney problems and was very anaemic. She was admitted to hospital and I really thought I was going to lose her or the baby. Our marriage had all been such a rush and after the events of the last few weeks there had been little time to think. Now I had time to think and pray, holding close to me the little blue dress she had worn at our wedding.

Peter was born in July and was a gorgeous child. It was only a matter of days after his birth that we packed him on top of mops and buckets and suitcases in our new car and made off to our new posting.

25. Mixed Missiles

I cannot remember with any degree of certainty how we came by our first house in Limassol. What is imprinted on my mind is the address, if nothing else, because of its anonymity. 'Turn left at Mario's clinic, then fourth turning right, Messiatonia Road'. It was a single-storey bungalow with a flat roof and a balcony with wrought iron railings. The family who owned it used to live at the rear of the house and had a rather attractive daughter, whose dowry it was. A very noisy donkey resided in the coarse, dry, waste ground that separated us from the third turning right. I never did discover who owned him, but many a warm and sultry night was made sleepless by his braying.

We spent happy evenings on the veranda, drinking the local wines, but during the day this was Peter's territory, where he lay in a yellow pram, kicking his legs and soaking up the sun. It was Peter in his pram that attracted the attention of our first visitor. The doorbell rang and an agitated man stood in front of me.

"I am ham ham ham ham..." he said, before drawing a breath. "I am hum ham ham ham ham ham..." he repeated, beginning now to sound like a machine. Finally, with superhuman effort, he exploded with the word "Hamilton".

Flight Lieutenant Hamilton and his wife had been all but high-jacked at the airport by a couple of Cypriots who were trying to recruit them as tenants. I could see the wife's face peering anxiously from the car and quickly grasped the situation. Her poor husband was almost incoherent as we rescued wife and babe from these sharks. At dinner in their new home, some weeks later, I hoped that the stammer might not be so bad, but it was, not the least because he worked so hard to overcome it. Particularly disconcerting was his use of every technique to pronounce a word, followed by its sudden replacement.

"I hope you like stu, stu, stu. I hope you like stu, stu, stu. I hope you like beef."

It was from this little house that Kerstin and I set out to make our wedding vows again, in the little Catholic Church at Akrotiri. It was here also that Kerstin told me the news that she was pregnant again and it was here that, in the dying days of the old Cyprus Republic, when Greek and Turk were wed in uneasy government, my infant son attacked me!

I worked some fifteen miles away at the Air Terminal in the main base at Akrotiri. The roster of five days followed by five nights contrived to give me a long weekend every two weeks but it was a punishing schedule, made worse by the long drive from Limassol to Akrotiri at daybreak and dusk. It was a long and lonely road which wound through the orange groves of the huge Phasourri plantation and the Greek Cypriot village of Kollosi. Unarmed and with my memories of the recent past still in my mind, it was always a pensive and reluctant departure and a happy homecoming. No more so than on this October day, because on the world stage the Cuban missile crisis was nearing its climax as the new and charismatic US President John F. Kennedy squared up to Nikita Khrushchev and the world held its breath.

Closer to home, a party was arranged which coincided with one of my weekends. It was to be held in a ski hotel in the Trudos Mountains. I was recounting the details to Kerstin whilst throwing Peter up in the air, when I suddenly had my own missile crisis as he came down finger first into my eye. The pain was excruciating and a visit to the doctor the following day resulted in an eye-patch and a driving ban. I did not know how to break the news when I got home that evening but Kerstin had already made up her mind that she was driving. Negotiating the winding mountain road in daylight was frightening enough but at night in a tiny Renault it was a challenge for the best. And Kerstin was eight months pregnant!

It is not the journey that stands out in my mind, nor the party that followed, but the sheer beauty of the scene which greeted our eyes the following morning. The pine trees reminded Kerstin so much of Sweden; their unique scent, mixed with the smoke and smell of wood fires, permeated the cabin. The snow-clad mountaintops and blue sky gave way to slate-coloured uplands and the blue sea beyond. The beauty of this scene and my marital bliss fought for supremacy in my emotions with a burning resentment and sense of impotence at the potential threat to it all posed by the political crisis taking place so many miles away. The strains of *Lili Bolero* heralded the Overseas Service of the BBC; Russian merchantmen carrying missiles to Cuba were approaching the blockade of American warships...

While military forces all over the world were on alert, parents looked helplessly at each other and their children as two men, far away, played 'thermonuclear roulette'. I was reminded of something my mother had said in the depths of World War II, which had come as a shock to my *Boys Own* and 'tomato ketchup blood' view of patriotism.

"I don't care who wins," she said. "I just want my sons back." Peter and his mother – with another baby not yet born – were mine. How dare these remote strangers trifle with our happiness? As we made our way down the mountain we heard the news. Khrushchev and Kennedy had reached an agreement. The missile crisis was over and I could concentrate once more on being a proud father and husband. But was I still a soldier?

There were just the two of us at Akrotiri; 'Nobby', a senior Flight Lieutenant, and me. Nobby was an ex wartime air gunner and a highly professional Mover. He did not get on well with everyone and had sacked the man whose post I filled, but he got on with me and adored Kerstin, who he called 'Liz'.

Nobby lived on the camp in an ex-officio married quarter and we worked very long hours. It was easier for him, but to be fair, he would look after late departures and really early starters and did most of the administrative work and preparation. If we had a lot of work during major exercises or needed leave, we would get reinforcements from the UK or from somewhere else in the Near East.

Nobby was a man of small stature with piercing blue eyes that, when he leant back on his heels and confronted his antagonist, could bring anyone down to size. He was great fun but a bit sensitive. He and his delightful wife Vi had a child of fourteen and a child of seven and shortly after Kerstin had Peter, Vi proudly announced that a third was on the way; so we became a family business.

We had lots of disagreements and fallings out, mostly to do with me exceeding my authority and almost all conducted through the medium of our log or diary. This proved to be compulsive reading for officers posted in from time to time to reinforce our little team but face to face we never argued or fell out. Well, perhaps there was one time. A man called Rovaroe was on Nobby's shift most of the time and they shared a mutual hatred of each other. Rovaroe was a dark-featured man of South American extraction with attitude. He actually knew his stuff but Nobby could never give him best.

It must have been the Spring because it was the first day of summer dress. Rovaroe and I were looking out of the window when Nobby climbed out of his Land Rover and walked towards the building. He was wearing the longest shorts and highest socks I had ever seen.

"Here he comes," says Rovaroe, "The big white hunter."

In his smartly-pressed bush jacket and armed with a clipboard, he strutted along, head held high and looking from side to side. One could easily imagine a tiger prowling on a nearby roof in awe of the White Man. I thought it terribly funny and told Nobby about it. He was incandescent with rage and with me; heaven knows what torture he subsequently visited on Rovaroe.

Nobby and Vi were to become our lifelong friends and our paths crossed many times. Then there was David, our second child. By the time David was born we had moved to an Army bungalow in Berengaria Village, a guarded and fenced military married quarters site, named after the lady whose name I had first encountered during my stay in Kyrenia Castle. I also remembered visiting an Officers' Club there with Paul in a previous life.

We were blessed here by the services of Miriam, our Turkish maid. It was she who insisted on having my rock cakes – an early attempt at cooking which turned out to be more rock than cake. We were convinced that she wanted them to throw at the Greeks. It was also Miriam who, during the one moment that I took my eyes of him, left open the kitchen door and allowed Peter to wander out. I heard the screech of brakes and a commotion. The distance from the dining room to the kitchen seemed to extend. Calling his name, I ran, sure of a disaster, corroborated by the open door and an oblivious Miriam on her knees, scrubbing. The long path and open gate are still etched on my memory, followed by the sight of Peter, hand-in-hand with a Turkish guard who was guiding him towards me.

I am sure I thanked the guard profusely and may even have offered a few consolatory words to the taxi driver, still in his car in a ditch, but in truth my pervading memory is one of enormous gratitude for the safety of my son. My biggest mistake was relaying this to Kerstin when I visited her later that day in the maternity ward of the hospital.

We stayed in Berengaria long enough to experience an uprising in nearby Limassol, which lasted for about three hours, involved the expenditure of thousands of rounds of ammunition and explosives but which resulted in the deaths of only three people, two by accident and the third from a heart attack. We felt safe enough inside our guarded compound but we sheltered behind an upturned heavy oak table for the duration. I don't think that was my idea, somehow, but that of the emerging Swedish General.

26. Mixed Messages

It is said that the message "send reinforcements we are going to advance" was relayed by word of mouth along the trenches in the First World War and understood by some blimpish general as "send three and fourpence we're going to a dance." No doubt this was the same general who asked an Aussie soldier "have you come here to die?" and got the reply, "nah, I came here yesterdie."

Whatever the truth of these silly yarns, the importance of good communications is a cardinal principle of war, or business if it comes to that, which is perilous to ignore. But there are dangers even for the most well-intentioned practitioner, not helped by codes, jargon and procedures. For myself, I have always been an advocate of clear speech. Ain't I?

This was graphically brought home to me when handing over my squadron of 'Bofors' guns in Jordan to a man called 'Dick' – an unfortunate name for someone in charge of the rude soldiery of the time. He was an ex-Army officer, which breed the RAF were inclined to favour, irrespective of previous experience. However, Dick had probably been in one of the administrative supporting corps, essential but not particularly warlike. There again, I was only a humble Flying Officer and he was a Squadron Leader.

No doubt he was conscious of, if not sensitive about, names in general and his in particular, so imagine his delight when he heard himself being described over the air as 'Sunray'.

"What's this Sunray business?" he enquired of the signaller on the first gun.

"It's the nickname for the Commanding Officer," the young man replied.

At the next gun position Dick went up to the man on the radio set. "What do the chaps call *me*?" he asked.

The radio man hesitated but Dick, smiled and reassured him. "That's right, what's *my* nickname?"

A smile creased the signaller's face. "Oh that," he responded. "Organ Features."

Sergeant Gibby was our only sergeant and the linkman on days in this very busy but tiny Air Movements Section at RAF Akrotiri. He was not very supportive of my attempts to get radios for our teams working on passenger and cargo aircraft arriving and departing this huge airfield. He eventually confided in me that he simply dried up over the radio. "Just speak plain English," I remonstrated. "Let's have no 'do you read me', 'over' or 'strength this or that'."

It was during the day and we had a particularly difficult aircraft to handle on a far away dispersal, a Pakistani Airlines Boeing 707, which had landed in an emergency. Good communication between the control office and the aircraft pan was vital.

"Take one of the sets, get down there and establish a radio link," I ordered Gibby. He went off sheepishly, climbed into the Land Rover and disappeared. Ten minutes later the receiver sprang into life.

"Sierra, Gulf, Tango Gibby here," it crackled, in best NATO phonetics.

"Bravo, Oscar, Sierra, Sierra here," I replied. "Prat."

'Gibbo' was good at handling passengers, he knew all the rules and applied them kindly, was pretty happy with his day job and a bit smug too. It was time to put him to the test. I rang from a remote telephone.

"Brigadier Bloodnock here..."

"Yes sir, Sergeant Gibby, how can I help you?"

"I want to take my orang-utan home with me to England."

"Oh, I am terribly sorry sir but live animals other than police dogs are not allowed on RAF aircraft," says Gibbo.

"Good God man! Damn thing's not live. Stuffed, don't you know," says me.

"That's fine," says a relieved Gibbo. "It can go in the belly hold as part of your baggage allowance."

"Nonsense!" exploded the brigadier (I was now fully 'in character'). "It goes in the seat next to me. Got no wife, no blasted kids, use hardly any of my allowance, least I can expect."

Pause...

"You must speak to my officer," says Gibbo.

Nobby's replacement was a pleasant but untrained young woman. I felt obliged to put Sgt Gibby on shift with the new officer.

Within days Mrs Gibby came to see me and convinced me that her marriage was doomed if he continued on shift. I gather this was prompted or inspired by a remark overheard in the Sergeants' Mess about 'Gibbo' spending most nights in a Land Rover with a female officer! More likely, it was to remove him from a punishing schedule. From then onwards, I was effectively always on duty. Thus are the seeds of disaster sown.

27. A Piss Pour Job

I would not wish to bore the reader with the complexities of air operations and military logistics. However, life-changing events took place at Akrotiri which may excuse a foray into this otherwise forbidden territory. The work there came more and more frenetic as military air transport operations at Nicosia were reduced and the 'bomber' base at Akrotiri became the major transport route station to the Far East. Until this point, our work was all about moving military passengers and cargo engaged on exercises and aero-medical evacuations from Akrotiri Hospital. Our operations staff did not readily grasp the complexities of general passenger handling or indeed the special needs of the Transport Command crews flying to international air transport rules and requirements.

In the local 'Movements' community there was huge resistance to transfer resources to us as the work came across. They had invested a lot of money and effort building up all the facilities in Nicosia and believed they could stop the inevitable. Perhaps they had forgotten, or tried to ignore that in the RAF it is the 'Air Staff' – essentially the flying element of the RAF – who always make decisions. So I was 'piggy in the middle', getting little support or sympathy from either side and, from some, what seemed to me like active opposition.

The work increased and aircraft originally scheduled to go to Nicosia came in to Akrotiri. Appeals for help were mostly ignored, indeed it was suggested that I was somehow complicit in the operational decisions to flow aircraft through Akrotiri. I tried to be loyal to my station, loyal to my specialisation at the headquarters and loyal to my team. Days spent wrangling for extra resources and trying to apprise my local commanders of the complexities of passenger movement whilst making do with what I had, were followed by long nights of physical work, preparation and supervision. Airfield opening hours, always flexible, were progressively extended and still there was no relief.

One dreadful night, I arrived at the airfield dispersal pan just past midnight to finalize the loading of a Britannia aircraft in the cargo role. Engineering equipment and boxes of spare parts had been presented by a visiting bomber squadron for loading, which, unbeknown to us, contained acid batteries. Work done and in failing light, I sent the loading team home and arranged to be back at six in the morning to see it off.

I slept badly, if at all, and at first light was in my Land Rover and down to the pan. The grey Britannia aircraft loomed up in front of me, still partly lit by the yellow phosphorous lamps. I pushed the aircraft steps a foot or so forward to gain access and soon was inside, making my way down the cargo, checking the general security of the load. Then I saw it. A trickle of fluid, a few feet long. I tasted the fluid and it was acidic – we had an acid spill to deal with! Planes are made of aluminium; acid reacts with aluminium and makes it porous.

I set my team to unload and called out the servicing engineers to carry out decontamination. There was much to do: alerting operations, delaying and cancelling the flight, diverting and accommodating the passengers, advising the headquarters whilst carrying on dealing with the continual flow of aircraft.

A local inquiry was convened, which established quickly that the batteries were incorrectly packed and labelled and were presented with the wrong paperwork. Furthermore, certificates had been given to say that no dangerous or hazardous cargo had been presented for loading. I was assured that no blame had been attached to me or my team.

Before the incident I had put my concerns in writing to my masters, to no avail. However, a little later, in response to an innocent question about my health from the Commander-in-Chief and his lady, prompted perhaps because I had boils, my arm was in a sling and their aircraft was slightly late, I thanked them for their concern, apologised for the delay and said that we were somewhat overstretched. This was an understatement, to say the least, but no doubt regarded as an act of disloyalty by my superiors. Or perhaps it was the inquiry itself which finally prompted action, but within days some hundred men and their officers were transferred from Nicosia to Akrotiri and the crisis was over. So was my career as the Senior Air Movements Officer.

My leader did not know what to do with me when he took over my job and plans for the future, so a scheme was devised to separate out the operational and exercise part of the organisation from the day-to-day administrative movements business. This gave me an element of independence but still left me dependent on him for any resources I needed to do the job. My unit was known as the Near East Mobile Air Movements Team. Then came the horses or, more precisely, the King's horses, but without the king's men.

The job of calling forward passengers and freight, previously done at Nicosia, was now transferred to the Headquarters Movements staff and away from the operating airfield. Perhaps had it not been so, wiser council might have prevailed, but when we were tasked to fly four Arab horses, a gift from King Hussein to our C-in-C, from Jordan to Cyprus, it was decided to give a selection of worthies the opportunity to enjoy a day's outing to Jordan.

The aircraft used was a Beverley, a monstrous beast, like a huge box suspended under a large boom. The box was used for cargo, the boom for about thirty passengers. The cargo in this case was to be the horses and the passengers, friends and families of favoured people. None of this was my concern but guess who was chosen to load the aircraft and travel with it to Jordan, collect the horses and fly back? You've got it, the Mobile Air Movements team.

From my days at 'Hab' and Manby I knew a little bit about horses. They pee and defecate rather a lot, usually at inconvenient times. Like acid battery juice, urine is corrosive, therefore some method had to be found to protect the aircraft floor. The best things I could come up with were large metal drip trays, lots of straw and numerous buckets. The obvious difficulty would be to keep the horses still and calm.

Enter the so-called Vet. I have no idea whether he was a Vet or just a spare cavalry officer whose wife, no doubt, was to enjoy a trip to Jordan in the boom above, but that is how he was sold to me. He also was the man who would supervise the loading and offloading of the horses and had drugs to quieten them.

I had not been back to Jordan since the days of 'Glubb Pasha', so I looked forward to an hour or so of sightseeing. The journey out was uneventful, except for an encounter with the 'Vet'.

"So, you've got the drugs to knock 'em out if they get difficult?" I said.

"Oh no," he quipped. "Just a penknife to cut the jugular. They would be dead in three minutes."

Dear reader, can you imagine the damage an enraged horse could inflict on an aircraft in that time? Not to mention that, like pee, blood is corrosive and horses have gallons of it.

We landed at what used to be RAF Amman, now looking somewhat run down. There followed a discussion of how to transport and return the civilian passengers and finally a coach appeared, which took us all to the city. I can recall little now of the sights and sounds. I looked for the Continental Hotel which the thrifty Scot and I had escaped from all those years ago but only remember coming across, in the souk, the famous John the Baptist, now called 'Jean Baptiste, Silversmith'. John was one of those merchants who had lived in the cantonment at Habbaniya and from whom I had bought various trinkets, all eventually lost to me by theft. I bought an armband from him for Kerstin before making my way back to the airfield.

When I returned to the aircraft, the horses were at the sill of the plane, accompanied by an Arab handler or '*sisse*'. He assured me that they had been tranquillised but were very lively. It was a tremendous struggle getting them to go up the ramp and tethering them to the side. Indeed, the last one was impossible to emplane and we had to leave it behind.

As the aircraft gathered speed down the runway and took off, the horses were restless, to say the least. The drip trays were soon filled to overflowing and at this point two of my team began to scoop up the urine from the trays with buckets and thence into a high-sided container. Sometimes they were able to catch it in mid-flow but not without some collateral damage. The flying time to Cyprus was about two hours but the route took us over Syria, with whom we were not best friends at the time.

Over Damascus we were asked for details of our load and, for reasons which I suspect were due to our passenger component, the Syrians kept us circling round Damascus for an hour whilst the horses got more and more agitated and I became increasingly convinced that we would all finish up in jail. Finally they let us go. Loud whinnying, snorting and the pounding of hoofs continued as the chaps fought valiantly with pail and tray, until the welcome sight of the island of Cyprus came into view.

"Well done," I said to my team, as the last horse clip-clopped off the aircraft.

"What a piss pour job that was," they said in unison.

Well... that's Movements.

Perhaps the Headquarters wanted to rub my nose in it but the next task was to return to Nicosia to handle the rotation of the Danish contingent of the United Nations Force, who arrived and left in a wave of Royal Air Force Britannia aircraft at hourly intervals. There was a problem of identification because so many were called Jorgensen, Jonsten or Smit. They were very happy because their first rotation had been care of the Italian Air Force, who, they maintained, must have had only one map or navigator between them, because they flew in formation. They were relieved to get the RAF this time.

All went well until the last aircraft took off. It had only reached a few thousand feet when the main cargo door seal started to leak. The Britannia was a pressurized aircraft and the noise when the seal blew was dreadful. The plane landed back at Nicosia some time later, after it had dumped fuel. The passengers, white and shaking, were taken off to a barracks for the night, no doubt saying 'come back Alfonso, all is forgiven.'

But for me the night was not over. At about two in the morning I was woken by a terrific thunderstorm and remembered that the aircraft steps had been left in position close to the plane. A strong wind could cause them to smash against the fuselage. Perhaps the writing off of one Britannia, care of acid contamination, persuaded me to do my best to save another.

The aircraft handling area or 'pan' was a vast open expanse of concrete, bathed in a weird yellow light from huge masts. I walked the distance with lightning playing all around me, rain teeming down and gusting wind. It was a struggle to do the job on my own but I went back to my bunk, albeit soaking wet, a contented man.

It seemed my son David was missing me, so the next day, instead of travelling back by car, I took a lift in an Army light aircraft. The pilot decided to scare the pants off me by doing aerobatics over the mountains and then flying as low as he could but it was with total sincerity that I shook his hand and thanked him for a super flight.

On 7th March, my birthday, three years to the day from setting sail from Southampton, we arrived home at Lyneham airfield. One of the perks of the trade was that we had our car with us. Our Renault 4L, with our baggage packed in it, trundled along the lanes of Wiltshire, en route to Hastings. The frost glistened on the grass and trees and made Christmas pictures of the little villages we went through. It was good to be back in England.

Granny was there for us, as usual, with beds made up and food on the hob. She was living in a small cottage close to the house my brother had bought at the end of the war but by now he had moved and she was a bit isolated. After our first night we went downstairs to find that, after giving up her bed to us, she was sleeping on a settee. The night before it had looked cosy enough but now the snow had penetrated the door and her head was resting close to it.

This was too much for Kerstin and me and within days we started looking for a more suitable house for her. We looked at three houses and she chose one of them, in the Old London Road. It was soon to become 'Granny's Cottage'. Close to the Post Office and the shops and free from any financial worry, it was all she ever wanted. My brothers and sisters and their children continued to visit and help her in any way they could and it became, for us, our first home.

Oh yes, and our first mortgage.

28. Days of Glory

My posting back home could not come soon enough and my new appointment was something of a surprise. I suspected I would get a job in some cosy Supply Depot, instead of which it was 'Movements' again, at a place called Colerne, close to the grand old city of Bath. Colerne was the home of the Hastings transport aircraft. There were two squadrons of them and a training wing. The Hastings was introduced just as the war ended. It was given a tail wheel and the nose stood well off the ground. It was apparently intended to carry a jeep slung underneath, although I never saw that done. By now, after the Berlin airlift, it was an old lady of the sky and with its steeply sloping floor and side door, any heavy cargo loading was literally an uphill battle and fraught with danger.

With the arrival in service of the Britannia, Argosy and Comet, collectively called 'The Shiny Fleet', the poor old Hastings was used only for parachute drops and for cargo and passengers on exercise. Any movements overseas were made via one of the major airfields, so no Customs or Immigration were required and little was on board these aircraft when they left or arrived – so why Movements? Well, it seemed that all this was going to change. In future the Hastings would load up and return directly to Colerne and I was to be the Movements officer.

This could be Akrotiri all over again. I had no men, no equipment, no office, no passenger terminal, but thankfully no 'Spartacus'. Clearly, I had to act quickly. Old passenger steps were soon acquired, plus a Land Rover with towing arm and a couple of flat trailers. Cargo handling access was achieved using two angled ramps attached to the side of the fuselage, which enabled a vehicle to be driven up to the top and then bounced around and into the aircraft. A larger ramp was available, which provided a sloping platform at the top of the two ramps that gave a little more manoeuvrability. It was much heavier and difficult to position and was itself not air transportable. There must be a better solution.

Once aboard the aircraft, cargo had to be secured to the floor to withstand a crash. A system of short, heavy steel chains was in use, which took an age to couple together into daisy chains to secure the load. I could not fathom why the long, light chains used on modern aircraft could not be used instead. Then there were the strainers, which attached the chains to the floor points. Really heavy and carted around in sandbags when not in use! Why not put them in beer crates? The problem of a passenger terminal and office was equally difficult but a quiet drive around the airfield revealed an empty single-storey Secco-type building with easy access to runway and taxiways.

By now I had managed to recruit a medically downgraded Air Loadmaster (these were men, and later women, who operated the winches from helicopters and took the responsibility in flight for passengers and air cargo). Air Loadmasters were often at war with Movements staff and it was fun to have one of them as one of us, so to speak. My band was further reinforced by first one and then another officer awaiting a Movements course. I had not enjoyed the luxury of such a course so had little compunction in using them. Lastly, I had posted in a handful of airmen and a couple of corporals, to give me the basis of a two shift system.

We had drawn the keys from the guardroom, opened up the old building, switched on water and electricity and were in business before the station administrative tycoons were aware of our presence. Into this hive of activity strode the Station Commander and his senior admin man, the latter beside himself with rage. The Commanding Officer was a dour Scot and ex-wartime bomber pilot called Alastair Mackie. He listened to my reasons and smoothed the ruffled feathers of his companion.

"I take your point and salute your initiative. You have done the right thing in the wrong way and now we have to regularise it."

I had my terminal and I had pleased the 'air staff'.

A few days later I was called to see the CO. The Group Captain bade me sit down at a desk in his office and handed me a file marked 'Inquiry'.

"Read it through and then we will talk about it," was all he said. It was an inquiry into the battery incident and made uncomfortable reading. The damage done to the aircraft was considerable, special praise being given to the engineering team who had apparently discovered the spillage! It was established that the fault lay squarely with the Bomber Command unit in the UK who had sent out the batteries in the first place.

Mention was made of my young WRAF officer and the fact that she was not responsible, as indeed she wasn't, but leaving hanging the idea that there was a problem which someone could have done something about. That someone should, it implied, have been me. Then, what really hurt was a comment by the CO of Akrotiri that an exceptional officer might have averted disaster, implying that Holland was in no way exceptional! The final nail was driven in by the Commander in Chief of Transport Command, Air Chief Marshal Sir Kenneth Cross, who, if memory serves, declared that "this fellow should never be allowed near a transport aircraft again except under supervision."

What a blow! What a document to hit me with, just days after my arrival at a new command. Furthermore, if I was so bad, why was I back as a senior Mover? Mackie looked up from his desk.

"Well Laddy, what do you think?"

I did my best to explain the events of a few months ago and my resentment at being blameless but slandered anyway, without having had the right to reply. I pointed out that the comments were unfair and unsupported.

Mackie pulled a face and said, "I believe that you could redress the C-in-C if you thought that, in the long run, you would achieve anything except notoriety."

The fact that, in spite of the comments of my old boss and new C-in-C, I was back doing Movements and that no blame had been attributed and no punishment awarded, may have contributed to my decision. Or perhaps it was a feeling that, whatever the cause, it had happened on my watch. Then again, it might have been my good old 'Catholic guilt' coming to the fore or maybe I just wanted to prove them wrong. Whatever it was, I decided to put it behind me and get on with life.

Mackie read every letter or signal which came to the base. For the next three weeks or so he would ring me most days and ask a question or seek clarification. This was just enough to make me think I was being watched. By some weird chance the very officer who had conducted the local inquiry into the acid spillage was now my specialist staff officer at Group Headquarters. He always tried to be chummy and distanced himself from the findings of the inquiry. To be fair, although he may have been responsible for some factual errors and omissions, he could hardly be blamed for the interpretation put on his findings by others.

Headquarters were also the people who called forward cargo and passengers to be embarked at my airfield. Late one afternoon I was advised that two rolls of cable were being despatched to be loaded onto a Hastings. The dimensions were passed to me and were quickly seen to be far greater than could ever be accommodated by a Hastings, so I refused to accept them. Signals and messages flowed but I was adamant there was no way I was going to risk lives, at night, attempting an impossible task.

Just after midnight I was called out to the Cargo Shed. Outside there were two staff cars, one with the CO's flag a-fluttering. Inside the shed, armed with clipboard and pad, stood the staff officer, next to the rather dapper figure of Alastair Mackie. Towering above them were two huge reels of coaxial cable. I greeted our visitor warmly enough and tried to hide my surprise at the presence of the CO.

"*Quad erat demonstrandum*," I uttered.

Mackie wrestled with the problem for a moment and then suggested we might cut the cable and put it on to four or more smaller reels. Before he had finished the sentence he realised that we had neither the expertise nor the equipment to do this. It was serious cable, almost a foot in diameter, and cutting it, even if possible, would have rendered it useless. The drums were loaded back onto a huge low loader and the matter was ended.

This marked the first victory in a comeback which featured the design, manufacture and adaption of loading equipment. I employed equipment from other aircraft, designed and had manufactured 'sledge pallets' and a dozen innovations, all of which I had to fight for against the dead hand of the design authority and aircraft safety regulations. Then there was the Zambian airlift, in which, with Southern Rhodesia being sanctioned, oil was being flown to Zambia. The 'shiny fleet' was fully committed to this operation and suddenly Colerne, with its aging aircraft, was a hive of activity, moving huge numbers of passengers and cargoes through to places worldwide.

I managed to convince the pilots and crews of the aircraft that any wish of theirs was our command, leading me, on one occasion, with a particularly difficult bunch, to fall down on my knees and worship as their aircraft taxied to a halt! The message got around the crew rooms pretty quickly that 'our Movers are a great bunch'. As for my team, I tried to keep them professional and tried to involve them in any development or 'workaround'. My own standing with my men was amply demonstrated one cold night when one of them asked if he might be personal.

Following the 'Organ Features' incident in a former life, I was forever reluctant to invite airmen to be personal, or to attend all-ranks parties or anything else which would make me hostage to fortune. However, that night, with my duffel coat up over my service cap and feeling for all the world like Jack Hawkins in *The Cruel Sea*, I took a chance.

"Do you know who you remind me of?" he asked.

"No," said I, already regretting my incautious offer.

"A f***ing pixie!"

I had established a good rapport with my boss, the Wing Commander in charge of air operations. One day he showed me a letter from headquarters which gave approval for one of my innovations. In the margin the CO had written: 'Perhaps we should recommend Holland for an award'. I assumed this was a monetary award under a new scheme which was only then being introduced and for which I held little hope of success. But it was another victory for a man who 'should not be allowed near aircraft on his own'! Some months later, a sealed, confidential letter arrived, asking if there were any nominations for honours and awards. Without really thinking, I irreverently scribbled 'Holland for the MBE' and returned it to my leader.

Our activities came to an abrupt halt one day when we learned that one of the aircraft had crashed. I have to admit that many times as I watched our heavily-laden planes disappear at the end of the runway, barely airborne before they seemed to drop into a valley towards the city of Bath, I used to hold my breath, waiting to see the silver flash of the wings as the aircraft reappeared.

With all our new-fangled ideas, sometimes only introduced after much argument and discussion with those responsible, the news that an aircraft was lost sent shivers down my spine.

We waited some hours before the awful news came through that the plane was carrying paratroopers and all aboard had perished. The whole fleet was grounded whilst investigations into the crash continued and it was months before repairs and modifications were introduced to allow a resumption of flying.

During this sad and prolonged period of inactivity, my next posting was announced. I was to join the Supply staff at the headquarters as a 'policy man'. The suggestion seemed to me preposterous. I knew nothing about supply policy. For the first time ever, I phoned up the postings department and asked if they had the right Holland. Surely, to get that sort of job would require me to be a very high calibre supply officer. It was quiet for a moment down the line before the officer informed me that I had the best annual report of anyone of my rank in the Service. I was sure they had the wrong man but, working on that assumption, I said that if I was that good, I should be on the Movements Staff. So it was that I became a Movements staff officer at Headquarters Transport Command Upavon, where my boss was Air Chief Marshal Sir Kenneth Cross.

Meanwhile, Kerstin was pregnant and we asked Granny up to Colerne to babysit should I need to take Kerstin into hospital. She was always good with the boys, who were now two and three respectively. When the time came Kerstin and I set out for the RAF hospital at Wroughton, about twenty miles away. It snowed and we slipped and slithered but made it to Wroughton with nerves a-jangle but otherwise in good shape. I stayed with Kerstin only long enough to settle her in and then returned to Upavon, Gran and the boys. I could barely contain my impatience when Kerstin phoned to say that the pains were very frequent and she was in labour.

An hour went by before I phoned the hospital and to my surprise the nurse announced that I had a lovely and healthy little girl. I somehow didn't expect a girl and when I told my mother we both just wept with joy and relief. Ingrid Kristina Marie was born and nothing would be quite the same again.

A week or so later I parked my car in the drive of our married quarter and rushed in to see 'Krissy'. I had lunch (staff officers could do that!) then went back to the car. It had gone. To my surprise I found it in the garage and wrapped round the bonnet was the garage door! 'Someone' had left the handbrake off!

When the station commander sent for me I had all my excuses ready. The slope of the drive was too steep, the garage door was too flimsy – it wasn't me.

"Stop," he said. "I don't even know about your damned garage door. I have asked you to see me so that I can tell you that you have been made a Member of the Order of the British Empire."

Mackie had been replaced by a man called Barratt, who I barely knew, so I spoke instead to my old Wing Commander boss. After thanking him I went on to say what a fantastic surprise it had all been.

"It shouldn't have been," he quipped. 'You asked for it!"

The first of many letters of congratulations I received told me how valuable my service had been and what an exceptional fellow I was. It was signed, Sir Kenneth Cross, Commander in Chief and meant more to me than I could ever explain.

A few years later, at Tengah in Singapore, I was to drive across the runway at midnight to meet two senior officers who were arriving in a Victor bomber. I didn't have to meet them, they were an operational crew and it was in the middle of the night but I was happy to do so and to take them to my newly furnished VIP lounge in what had been described in a recent Ministry publication as 'the miracle Movements centre of the Far East'. Out stepped Air Marshal Barratt, who was quick to notice that, in the dark, I had put on my medal ribbons upside down.

"I would not have given you that," he said, "if I thought you wouldn't wear it properly."

His manner softened over a gin and tonic. His companion, a dark, swarthy individual, looked at me in a quizzical fashion, the same look he had given me at Manby when I was an RAF Regiment Flying Officer and he a young Wing Commander, the same look he had given me at RAF Akrotiri when I tried to explain to him the complexities of Air Movements and sought his help. Whether he realised it or not, Air Chief Marshal Sir Peter Horsley had just completed the circle. Oh, and Alastair Mackie, I heard he became Vice Chairman of CND!

If there is a moral to this story, it must be to think long and hard before railing against the system or – as the District Officer looking for a missing missionary said to the cannibal chief he found puking on the floor...

"You can never keep a good man down."

29. A Family at War

The Lord Chancellor's office had told us to be there early and the chaos caused by a new railway timetable, as we had battled up to London from Wiltshire the day before, had underlined the wisdom of this advice. We had done it in style and had spent the previous night at the RAF Club, my mother, Kerstin and me, our little family left in the care of my sister Wendy, as surprised as me by the whole event and anxious to help her little brother and his child wife! My mother dressed in blue, with all the grace and dignity of the Queen Mother she admired so much. Kerstin, in a large silk hat and wispy chiffon dress, all yellow and light green, looked delightful and so very young.

Only a few days before, a disinterested shop assistant had asked what madam wanted, suspecting madam was even younger than she looked.

"I need something to go to the Palace in," she had said.

The reaction was truly remarkable and the scene that followed had all the ingredients of a far-fetched film fantasy so common at the time. The manageress was called and a team of helpers dressed her, first in this, then in that. Hats were considered, compared with shoes and bags until, almost without a word from Kerstin, she was dressed for the occasion and thrilled with the result.

Now here, we were strolling through St James's Park to the Palace with a lot of time to waste. Self-conscious in uniform, I felt abashed to be the centre of attention and almost guilty about the red and white ribbon of the Order of the British Empire which stood out on my new blue serge. Despite all the fuss caused recently by a similar award to the Beatles, I kept thinking that, for military men, awards were for bravery. What had I done worthy of such a distinction, except to load aeroplanes better than most?

It was at a place called Ramadi, on a bend in the river Euphrates, that my father saw the horror of war for the first time. He had joined the Army as a man, although only a boy of fourteen. Army life must have been fun after working from the age of eight at Lister's Mill in Bradford, but service in Britain and India could not have prepared him for what he was about to see.

The Euphrates presented a natural barrier to the army of General Maude, on the long, hot route across the Black Desert to retake Jerusalem in this last great crusade. The Turks were courageous fighters, the British, in full kit, boots, helmets and spine pads, advanced relentlessly over one of the hottest places on earth. It seems a feint assault was to be made by several thousand men to divert the attention of 'Johnny Turk' from the main attack to be launched elsewhere.

My father, now a Battery Sergeant Major in the Royal Artillery, was ordered to establish a forward observation post from which he could direct the fire of the guns. This in itself is dangerous employment but in those days the only means of seeing properly was to climb a ladder. Ladders are not part of the desert landscape and tend to be noticed. It was hardly surprising that his call for a volunteer fell on sensibly well closed ears. Gritting his teeth, he climbed. What he saw from his vantage point appalled him and remained with him to his deathbed, from which he recounted the tale to me.

Thousands of men were simply slaughtered by withering machine gun fire, the river red with blood. He said little of his work up the ladder or the flesh wound that brought him down to earth with a bump, but he was mentioned in dispatches and was commissioned in the field in his own Royal Regiment. The story he told me that night explained the excitement he had expressed when I had written to him from the sprawling RAF base in Iraq several years before.

'It is on a bend in the river,' I had written, 'not far from a lake called Habbaniya and between two towns, which must be as old as time itself. One is called Fallujah, the other Ramadi'. He had his day of glory, a commission in his own regiment for 'Laddie' Holland, the boy from Bradford, but today he would share in mine.

Poor George had no glory that we know, no reward for his self-sacrifice, just the deprivation of a prison camp, a diet of rice, which he hated, and death when the war was finished on the wretched railway he had helped to build, the railway which cost a man's life for every sleeper laid through the thick jungle of Siam.

George was my parent's first child, born in India, better educated than most and fastidious in his ways. Steadfast and loyal, he worshipped my father and provided the stability needed in such a large family. At twenty he started to go blind. A brain tumour was diagnosed and the prognosis was bleak. As fate would have it, a young surgeon called Cairns, with a new and untried technique, offered to operate. George leapt at the chance to regain his sight, unaware that death lurked close behind.

An appointment was fixed and George was admitted. On the day of the operation, the family – there must have been eight or more – awaited news of the outcome into the late evening, unaware that, for several hours, a telegram had lain unopened on the doorstep which said simply 'operation successful'.

This all happened before my arrival on the scene to complete the family but, at the age of six, I watched while my brother George, home on leave, berated my parents for interfering with his life. They had told the Army about his medical history. He was 'off the boat' because of them. Why could they not leave things as they were? Why indeed?

Who knows what strings he pulled or lies he told but the next memory I have of events was that he was going back to where he had been born. This could only mean India. A pawl of depression settled over what remained of our family when news that George was missing reached us. Singapore had fallen and the 18th Division, of which he was part, could only destroy their equipment and surrender.

Hope returned when we learned that he was a prisoner of war but those little printed cards, courtesy of the Imperial Japanese Army, gave no insight into the horror of it all. All the prayers were to no avail. I did not need to be told, when I saw my father sobbing, that gentle and kindly George was gone. The surgeon's knife had saved him for a crueller fate.

He too, must share my day.

Of course you do not have to die to suffer in war. Albert, my professional soldier brother, was with the 8th Army in North Africa, at Salerno and throughout the Italian campaign. Whilst Ray, who joined when he was barely old enough, was to meet him in Rome, after several months pinned down on the Anzio beachhead. He went on after the war to serve in Palestine.

These two must also share my day.

So also must Fran, the only other member of my family to be in the RAF. A Flight Sergeant Balloon Commander, she was scarred by a girl digging her nails into her hand in fear during an air raid on Hull. Her life was full of tragedy. She lost her fiancé, a bomber pilot, and, I was to learn many years later, would end the war in despair, badly treated by a man, by the Service she loved and by the prejudices of the time. She too must share my day.

Working with the RAF as a nursing sister, Wendy spent the war on operational flying stations such as Tangmere. She met the 'aces' and nursed the burned and crippled airmen. Her treasured possession is a model Spitfire in brass, mounted on a piece of a 'prop', presented to her by her patients. Pat also served as a WREN. Always a blonde delight, she must have cheered up the Senior Service, even if she sank no U-Boats!

The waiting and the deprivation at home was not so good either. My eldest sister Biddy, when not escorting wounded soldiers in her VAS role, was at home fixing things, getting fuel, looking after the remaining children, sharing the tension and the waiting with my mother and father. Hers was not an easy task, no glamour for her, just hard work.

These too must share my day.

As we walked towards the Palace I told my mother my thoughts. It was to be a family award.

"I think that's nice," she said, and I know this was her proudest day. A few hours before she died, she smiled and squeezed Kerstin's hand at the memory of it.

30. The Foursite Saga

Kerstin's English continued to cause amusement. We went through a phase when things 'said' things rather than 'went'. This was well illustrated by the gas oven affair. Kerstin was several months pregnant and struggling to make a meal. Unfamiliar with gas, she turned it on before hunting for the matches. I arrived shortly afterwards to find a tear-streaked, eyebrowless, eyelashless wife.

"I turned the bloomin' thing on and 'pouff' it said," was all I could get out of her. She's never liked gas since.

Her English improved and she spoke with gradually increasing confidence, developing an interrogative style of speech which has characterised her conversation ever since. I first noticed this peculiarity during an urgent and intense discussion with a NAAFI manageress on the unlikely subject of hearthrugs. It went like this:

Kerstin: "What are they made from?"

Manageress: "Sheepskins."

Kerstin: "How many sheepskins?"

Manageress: "Two."

Kerstin: "Do you have any rugs made of four skins?"

Self, under breath: "Just a little excitement and we can cover the lounge."

Manageress exits, somewhat embarrassed.

By now her dictionary had been discarded and her frankness on the one hand and naivety on the other made her vulnerable to my particular brand of humour. No doubt some might think this cruel and I take no pleasure in the telling of it. However, in so far as what follows reflects more on the stupidity of others than on her, I will indulge in just one further tale.

I suppose it started when we spent a few weeks living apart following my arrival at Hartlebury, while waiting for a married quarter. Living in the Mess is not a bad existence but one is invariably attracted to the bar in the evenings. In the interests of preserving my chastity I let it be known to the other mess members that I was married, knowing that this would quickly communicate itself to everyone on this closely-knit base and most especially to one young lady who was 'coming on strong', as they say. To add spice to the story I added that my wife was an alien. Interest immediately flared. More so when, after much probing, which I actively encouraged and, thinking back perhaps to my mother's mud hut theory, I let slip that my wife was an African princess.

I detected disappointment, mingled with an undisguised sense of relief, when my princess made her first appearance, although the fact that she was Swedish did cause a flurry of interest, especially amongst the wives, all of whom were old enough to be her mother. Amongst these was one particular wife, there always is, who felt that as the most senior officer's wife and because the commanding officer was a widower, she must take the lead. This of course means that she, let's call her Mrs 'S', must know everything before anyone else on the base.

I should perhaps explain that Hartlebury was a supply depot, criss-crossed with railway lines and bursting with equipment in innumerable sheds on seven different sites. Each site was a unit in itself and I commanded No.4 Site. This enabled me to make funny remarks about my site in what I described, with apologies to Galsworthy, as 'The Foursite Saga'. The decision had been made to close the depot and great uncertainty lay over its future and that of the many civilians working there. Not that this stopped one wag from replying, when the visiting Defence Minister asked how many people worked there: "About half of them, sir."

It had been a long Guest Night, with the local MP and dignitaries present. I just wanted to fall into bed and sleep.

"Who was there?" asked Kerstin, when I finally made it home.

I quickly ran through the main guests.

"What did they say?"

'Tell her something, anything,' I thought, as I fought to prevent the waves of sleep from taking hold.

"They were discussing plans for the future use of Hartlebury," I lied.

"And what will they do with Four Site?"

I made a supreme effort to keep awake, whilst telling her that the London Rubber Company was to take over the site to build a contraceptive factory there. The population explosion in the Far East had now reached such tremendous proportions that only radical action could save the world from disaster. The huge sheds and the railway network linked to the main line would enable the rapid distribution of the goods by the container load to the Orient.

At last she was quiet and sleep overtook me.

I left early next morning and by lunchtime the pain in my head had subsided and I was ready for my meal. I tried her tactic for once.

"How was the coffee morning?"

"Oh it was fine, nobody knew about the contraceptive factory, except of course Mrs 'S', who said that she had known about it for some time."

My open sandwich failed to connect with my open mouth as I searched her face for any hint of humour. There was none. I was hoist by my own petard!

The story went round the depot like wildfire, with many double entendres. Nobody was prepared to deny it as a hoax or tell it as it was, because to do so would have made the senior officer's wife look even sillier. Better to let the rumour circulate until overtaken by something new, if not more bizarre. I have no doubt that efforts were made to 'protect' the station commander from the story but, some days later, he quietly expressed the view that my site was a 'condominium'.

The upshot of it all was that my bluff had been painfully called but Kerstin emerged as the ill-used heroine of the piece and her popularity soared to new heights, at least amongst the men-folk.

Did she believe the story herself? I really don't know, but I took no chances in the future.

'A horseman'. Dad. circa 1912.

Peter, Portland, 1937.

Peter and Paul, Woods Farm, 1940.

Chelmsford, 1939.

Hastings, 1951.

Wakefield, 1943.

RAF Digby, 1952.

Gunner Instructors Course. Self front, second from right.

Pre OCTU, Catterick 1954. Self back row, last on right.

OCTU, Jurby 1954. Self front and right, with baton.

Passing Out Parade, Jurby, Isle of Man, June 1954. Self centre.

Sergeants' Mess, Deversoir, Eygpt. Self middle row, left.

Eygpt – With the Boss, Squadron Leader FC Aston, DFC.

Rugby, Officers and Sergeants v The Men, 'Right Dress'. Christmas 1954.

Rugby. Improperly Dressed, Christmas 1954. Self centre.

Rugby. The Officers and Sergeants, Christmas 1954.

Officers and Dogs. Self centre back, behind Wg Cdr Bill Elliot, Habbaniya 1955.

Soldiers in Blue, Habbaniya 1955.

'Chico Sahib', with apologies to
the Arab Legion.

'To Horse', Habbaniya 1956.

Why the long face? Manby 1956.

'No Stirrups', Manby 1957.

Friendly Quartermasters, Manby 1957.

SS *Nevasa*.

Kerstin and Peter, Cyprus 1962.

The Christening, Cyprus 1962.

Loading The Hastings, Colerne 1966.

A Family Award, Buckingham Palace 1967.

Upavon Ball, 1968.

OC ATMA Tengah, Singapore 1972.

A VIP Inspection, Singapore 1973.

The Air Terminal Airfield Side. Tengah, Singapore 1972.

Queensland Australia 1972.

Crewing for Peter, Singapore 1972.

Kristina Tree Hugging, Babi Tengah Island 1973.

'Gone Native', Babi Tengah Island, Malaysia 1973.

Goodbye to our friends, Babi Tengah Island 1973.

Ann-Marie reflecting, Brampton 1980.

'Then there were four', Hastings 1982.

'Funny Girl', Ann-Marie in Hastings, 1982.

'On yer bike!' Sergeants Mess, Henlow 1983.

Kristina with cannonball re-enacting 'Escape and Evasion',
Kyrenia Castle 1999.

A Family Wedding – Centre Left Ann-Marie (Bridesmaid), Kristina, Elizabeth (Bride), Peter, Self, Kerstin, David, surrounded by brothers and sisters. St Clement Danes 1989.

Christmas in Singapore, 1973.

Christmas at Henlow 1982.

'There's my Sleigh'. Ann-Marie and Kristina, Christmas at High Wycombe, 1984.

The Third Generation, William and Peta, Christmas 2010.

The Third Generation, Matthew and James, Christmas 2010.

Santa Lucia, Singapore 1972.

Santa Lucia, Kristina and Ann-Marie, 1988.

Santa Lucia, William and Peta, 2009.

Post Retirement. Millennium Ball, RAF Honnington 2000.

'I remember it well, I think' Cartoon by Rob Van den Top.

The Author, 2010.

31. Up the Slippery Pole

I next found myself posted to Strike Command Administrative Headquarters or SCAR, which was collocated with Fighter Group Headquarters at Bentley Priory, a huge old mansion in extensive grounds, once frequented by Lord Nelson and Lady Hamilton. Just inside the main door was a beautiful room with a remarkable ceiling, created in the 19th Century for the Dowager Queen Adelaide, who was bed-ridden.

Adjacent to the building was the underground bunker from which the progress of the Battle of Britain had been monitored in 1940, when Fighter Command was located there. In those days operations themselves were, of course, controlled by the Fighter Command Groups but by now, with the air force shrinking, there was only one Fighter Group and Fighter Command no longer existed.

My job required me to obtain spare parts for grounded unserviceable aircraft. We were required to work closely with the engineering staff but they were at High Wycombe. Furthermore, they were organised as specialists, by aircraft type, for example the Lightning fighter or the Victor bomber. We on the other hand, were organised by type of spares, for example engines and engine spares, aircraft spares, hydraulic spares, tyres, so that we matched the staff at the provisioning branches in the Ministry of Defence and the various supply depots. In my view this was not a good way to operate and the whole system needed to be reorganised from top to bottom. In my first months at SCAR I wrote a paper urging this course of action. It was not to happen for twenty years!

There were no married quarters available, so Kerstin and the children stayed with Granny in the little house in Hastings we had bought for her when we returned from Cyprus. It was summer and my brothers, sisters and offspring were used to staying with her during this time. Granny was never good at saying 'no' to anyone and even worse at dealing with more than one family at a time, so life for Kerstin was pretty rough for a while and, to compound everything, her own granny (*Mormor* in Swedish) died and the letter went astray. Eventually a truce broke out and the children went to the nearby convent school.

In contrast, I lived in the old mansion house during the week, returning to Hastings at weekends. I met up again with my old friend Hugh, an ex-Army major now Squadron Leader, who had shared the pain of the basic supply course with me although, as an ex-Army Ordnance Corps Officer, he was more familiar with 'supply' than I could ever be. We drank a lot and philosophised a lot and laughed a lot.

I wanted to recount an event to him which had occurred one Friday evening when I was getting ready to leave for Hastings. Officers of the Women's Royal Air Force (WRAF) had always had their own separate living accommodation but now they were to be known as 'Royal Air Force, brackets 'W', close brackets' and in this 'new age' there was to be no distinction in respect of jobs or accommodation.

My bags were packed and I was ready to go when there was a knock on the door and when I opened it, to my surprise, I beheld a scantily-dressed vision of loveliness.

"My hairdryer is broken," she pouted. "Have you got a screwdriver?"

"Phillips?" I asked.

"I don't care who's it is," she responded.

I resisted the temptation to linger and lust. Perhaps at least some of the old rules were right after all.

I went off for ten days leave with Kerstin, the children and Granny and returned, hoping to recount this yarn to Hugh. I asked after him in the bar but there was a shocked silence. The barman haltingly told me that Hugh had died suddenly and had been buried the previous week.

Not for the first time I felt my mortality and longed to be with my little family again.

Fortunately, shortly afterwards we were allocated a house on the outskirts of Watford. On the Monday morning we followed a trail of children to discover the closest school and signed them up. It was some months before we were allocated a house on base and moved the children's school once more!

To gain promotion you must be noticed for the right reasons or not noticed at all and you must also pass your promotion examinations. My advancement to Flight Lieutenant had been on the basis of undetected crime and the promotion examination for officers in the RAF Regiment. I had now been noticed for the right things but required success in the Supply Officers Promotion Examination for Squadron Leader.

The Regiment stuff had all been factual but, perhaps trying to move with the times and be more searching, the Supply papers made statements and asked you to discuss them. Worse still, the statements were often based on articles from various publications and newsletters where facts and opinions might be at odds, with some written by people who were misinformed or just plain wrong.

I had taken the wretched examination several times before my new boss at Bentley Priory, to his great credit, finally taught me the necessary technique in learning and reproducing the right sort of drivel to achieve success. My friend and colleague Chris was convinced that my failure was due to the fact that I had 'given up trying' after being awarded the MBE. Not true, I tried very hard, even living in the Mess to study in quiet, away from the kids. To recount it all here would be very boring; suffice it to say that in my view the exams themselves were flawed.

I passed at last, along with my good friend Tim, who had experienced similar difficulties. His wife made a lovely dinner and we celebrated together, hoping that soon we would be promoted. Finally, no doubt due to Kerstin's influence with my Group Captain's wife (or so she believed), within two weeks I was promoted and posted to Singapore.

There was a glitch, however. We all had the many 'jabs' needed but Kerstin had an adverse reaction. That sounds pretty tame but in fact her face erupted into numerous pustulating blotches. I was sure that smallpox could not have looked worse. Doc Ryan, our local GP, invited me to join him in poring over medical tomes that showed horrific pictures of unpronounceable ailments until finally admitting defeat. Kerstin was referred to the Hospital For Tropical Diseases in Soho where she was diagnosed as suffering from *erythema multiforme,* which I believe is a description rather than an ailment. We were told to go and get lunch somewhere and had a bizarre experience. The restaurant was fairly full and we made our way to a table, from which the people immediately got up and left. Nobody else came near us except the waiter, who did so with obvious trepidation, so we had a very quiet meal and our bill and change were delivered as quick as a flash. No attempt was made to encourage us to stay a moment longer than necessary.

The hospital wanted photos, no doubt to join the sort of gallery I had seen with Doc Ryan, so Kerstin was sat in front of an old fashioned plate camera. The photographer put his head underneath the cloth and was ready to do his stuff when Kerstin stopped him.

"What do you want now?" he said, rather grumpily.

"Let me know when you are going to take it," says Kerstin.

"Why?" says he.

"So I can smile!"

Within a few days her face started to improve and by the time we were packed up and ready to go she was almost back to her pretty self.

32. Somewhere East of Suez

The excitement of promotion to Squadron Leader was only matched by that of going to Singapore. From the age of seven, when my brother George was interned by the Japanese only hours after he got there, I had been intrigued by the story of the fall of Singapore. Now, after arriving at RAF Changi, the whole family and most of the passengers from our aircraft were put up in a downtown hotel of sorts called The Morningside Guesthouse. Apparently it had been a minor Japanese headquarters during the war and before that a British one. The only evidence I have of this came via an old servant who claimed to have told British officers that the Japanese were coming in through the jungle, thought by the British to be impenetrable. Did he, or had he read it later in a book?

We were given a large room with huge ceiling fans and several beds. The bedding was dubious and the pillows, although under clean pillowcases, revolting. A smell of damp oozed from every cupboard and corner of the room but the children were happy and very excited and I was able to slip down to the bar and try out some 'Tiger' beer.

I fell into conversation with an Army sergeant who mixed me up with the only other Squadron Leader on the flight, who happened to be a dentist. Drinks with other ranks has its own special dangers but when he came up close and asked if I could 'help him professionally' I – at that moment being unaware of his confusion – agreed without hesitation.

"It's this one back here," he said, sticking his finger in his mouth. "It's been givin' me gyp for days."

I could have got away with it at that point by telling him I was not the dentist, but I didn't.

"Come out here under the light and kneel down," says I, "so that I can get a good look. Now which one is it?"

His hand now almost entirely in his mouth, he looked up at me with baleful eyes.

"Can oo fee it?"

"Can't understand what you are saying," says I.

He swallowed hard and said "thiff one," poking his index finger to the back of his mouth.

I might still have got away with it if I had owned up then, but some self-destruct mechanism drove me on.

"I see it, that's no problem at all, but it will have to come out".

He now recovered himself slightly and said: "Can I come to your surgery tomorrow?"

"Not necessary, I can do it now," I said. "Let me just pop upstairs and get my pliers. I'll have it out in no time."

The man fainted.

"Wake up," I said (not a good idea with me still in the bar) adding as he stirred, "I'm not the dentist," (an even worse idea).

"You Bastard, I'll kill you!" he yelled, and struggled to get to his feet. By the time he did, I was already two floors up, door closed and hiding behind my family, my career as a dentist over for good.

The following day I dressed in a bush jacket I had bought from someone in the UK. It was made of very light material and looked smart if not quite the right shade of KD. I was picked up by an Australian Flight Lieutenant called "Butch" who had hands like hams and a handshake to go with it. I took to him immediately, perhaps because I was not used to the respect given to me by virtue of my new rank.

We went to a beautiful white colonial building with large pillars and a lot of marble, I believe it was called 'Temple Mead'. A conference was being held about the future of ANZUK Movements, chaired by a Marine Lieutenant Colonel and attended by about 20 majors, Butch and me. "You know Sir," he confided. "The population of Singapore is made up of 30 percent Chinese and 70 percent British Army Majors."

RAF Changi, with all its facilities, which included a route hotel called 'Changi Creek', was to close and RAF Tengah, a fighter base, was shortly to be handed over to the Singapore armed forces. After this an Australian, New Zealand and United Kingdom (ANZUK) Movements organisation would be established to handle all the military transport aircraft of the three countries. All would be solved when Changi closed down and some men and all the equipment were sent across. Sound familiar? I was to command ANZUK Tengah with a number of officers and men from the nations.

Command and control arrangements were odd. I was responsible to each of the three support unit commanders for the operational handling of their aircraft and the command of their men allocated to me. I was under the command of the RAF Wing Commander commanding the RAF Support Unit (RAFSU) but I was professionally responsible to an Australian Wing Commander who commanded the ANZUK Movements headquarters and booking centre at the naval base. The RAFSU commander regarded himself as the senior of the lot but they all thought otherwise. He, in turn, was responsible to Commander RAF Singapore, who worked in the naval base with the Senior RN Officer Singapore, together with... need I go on? I indented for a rollover noticeboard which showed me and mine responsible to each person likely to claim us in turn as they visited. It never arrived, but news of it made the point.

Our bungalow was away in the jungle. It had three bedrooms and amah's quarters outside. There were no windows in the house, just wooden slats, except for the front room, which had glass doors leading out onto a covered patio. There was a fair-sized garden, with bamboo, banana trees, orchids and some stately palms and we were hemmed in by monsoon ditches. Our road was called 'Vampire Road' and opposite was a 'Frankenstein Hanger', next to the bomb dump. Doesn't sound too good, does it? But for all that it was lush and beautiful, especially when enhanced with yellow fluorescent lighting.

One afternoon we held a joint birthday party for David and Kristina. Little tables overloaded with food were dotted around the gardens, waited on by Officers' Mess waiters. Afterwards, attempts at children's games were replaced with dancing when someone switched on the hi-fi and tuned in to the 'rock 'n' roll' music so popular at the time. The kids loved it and within minutes they were all up dancing and having a terrific time. Parents arriving to collect them were served drinks and the party went on and on until dark, with everyone joining in the fun.

Towards the end of our time in the bungalow, we invited the new RAF wing commander, who had arrived out only the day before, to come along to a soirée. It was one of the only times in my life that I saw someone experience what has become popularly known in latter years as 'the wow factor'. Straight out from the UK, where he and his wife had probably experienced little more opulence than a Mess Summer Ball, their first sight was the gorgeous floodlit Empress Palm. The veranda, bathed in light, led out onto the lawn, which was dotted with candlelit tables, where white tunic'd waiters dispensed drinks to our international guests.

Before we discovered floodlighting, the Empress Palm had provided me with refuge to prevent my mortal form from being discovered as we celebrated our first Christmas in Singapore. The pattern for our festivities had been pretty well established by this stage of our married life. After dinner on Christmas Eve I would complain bitterly about the absence of Father Christmas, saying that I had never seen him and I doubted if he existed. The children would all spring to Santa's defence and I would reluctantly go off to seek him out. I would make a leisurely exit through the front door, followed by a frenetic rush around the house and into the back for a change into costume, a rouging of the face, a shrinking of the frame and re-appearance at the front door – in character. I would later reverse the process and return, shaking my fist and professing astonishment at all the gifts and toys.

This Christmas was no exception. The amah's room, minus amah, provided me with my dressing room and, when I thought I had done a pretty good job of subterfuge and deceit, I made my way around the garden to the veranda. Suddenly, a truck drew up at the gate, in the back of which were numerous raucous, beer-swilling Australians telling each other it was Christmas. Two guys got out, one with a white beard hooked on his ears and a red hat. The other, as I remember, had a red scarf and hat. Both carried cans of 'Fosters'.

"Ho, Ho, Ho!" They shouted. Our veranda door opened and there was the family. Peter, who already had his doubts about the whole Father Christmas thing anyway; David, who was more interested in the contents of the sack than folklore; Kristina, whose belief in the little old man was total and Kerstin, who was responsible for the whole annual sick-making charade in the first place.

Momentarily off my guard, I jumped behind the nearby palm, at first determined to wait it out. But the Aussies were very drunk and I did not want the concept destroyed for all time, so I decided to act decisively. Out from behind the palm I sprang, and launched into a full-on verbal assault on these pretenders.

"He is not Father Christmas!" I shouted. "They are impostors. I am the real Father Christmas!"

Kristina was to tell me afterwards that she had seen Santa's reindeers on the roof of the bungalow that night and David and Peter were to deliver a torrent of words trying to relate what had taken place. I enjoyed the teasing and the fun. But what of the two Aussies, who had shrunk away back up the path and quietly, I hesitate to say soberly, climbed onto their truck? I like to think that to this day they tell their grandchildren about the day in Singapore that they really did see Father Christmas.

33. A Matter of Approach

One of my most treasured possessions is a thin blue leather-bound book called 'Customs of the Service'. Written by one Group Captain A. H. Stradling OBE and published in 1939, it gathers and explains within its pages the traditions, customs and practices on which the Service was based and offers advice to young officers on how they should behave both socially and professionally. It remains a snapshot of a pre-war, elitist Service in a simpler and more innocent world.

It was issued to me in 1954 at the Officer Cadet Training Unit at Jurby and provided invaluable information on social etiquette such as 'calling', the use of visiting cards and behaviour in the mess. It enabled me to understand, for example, that when one 'called' on the wife of the Station Commander, to be told by the servant that the lady was not 'at home', you refrained from saying, "Yes she is, I can see her hanging out the washing in the back garden!"

On the subject of leadership was the advice that you should treat a man like a valuable hunter (horse). That is, in the stable as if he was worth a hundred guineas and in the field, half a crown! As to criticism meted out by one's own superiors, one should be philosophical and complacent about it and remember the story about the native chief who, when accused of eating a missionary was violently sick, so proving that you can't keep a good man down (I knew I got it from somewhere!).

Hardly surprising that, being commissioned from the rank of corporal, a rank in which you live cheek by jowl in the barrack room with those you have to command, I did not find this helpful, or the transition easy, when dealing with my juniors or seniors, always expecting more from both than I was ever likely to get from either. In Singapore I was reminded of all this when Robbie ramrodded and crunched to attention.

I had met Robbie briefly on arrival. He had recently been commissioned and was awaiting an officer's Movements course. He was a Scot, seemed a pleasant and useful sort of chap and I looked forward to his return to join me after his training. However, when he did, something had changed. The previous evening I had watched him preparing an aircraft load for despatch and noticed that he spent most of his time stripped to the waist and driving a forklift truck. I decided to give him some advice about management.

I had hardly started to point out that if he behaved like a forklift operator then that is how he would soon be treated, and so on, when he stopped me abruptly to explain his dilemma. He said that when he had returned to England for his training he was attached to the Air Movements Squadron at Brize Norton. On his first day there he was told to report to the Senior Air Movements Officer (SAMO). He had crashed to attention in much the same way as he had just done to me. The SAMO feigned shock, falling back in his chair; he then told Robbie to sit down and relax. He was an officer now and should not give way to those parade ground urges so reminiscent of army sergeant majors, in which one tries to put one's foot through the floor in a misguided attempt to show unswerving and undying respect for one's senior, who was now lolling in a chair in front of one. Robbie got the message and, after a pleasant chat, left to go on his course.

Two months later he was called back to see the SAMO. Relaxed and bronzed from his recent outdoor activities, Robbie was a new man. So much so, that when he came through the door with a "Hi" and more of a friendly wave than a salute before falling down into a welcoming chair, the SAMO didn't recognise him, became incandescent with rage and physically threw him out of his office, telling him to go forth and learn some respect.

"OK Robbie," I said. "Just wear your shirt in future".

One way or another, I had been there myself. After all, it was not that long ago that I had returned the winks and nods of a shell-shocked army colonel aboard the good ship *Nevasa*.

The title *Customs of the Service* had been changed after the war to *Customs of the Services* to reflect the joint service commonality and applicability of the content. Indeed, I would have thought there were rather more 'hunters' in the Army than in either of the other two services. However, 'Stradling' had nothing to say about the customs, traditions or national characteristics of our Commonwealth brothers, as I was soon to learn.

Now, broadly speaking, my Australian contingent were brash, had an ambivalent attitude towards discipline and regarded being what they called 'laid back' as a vital component of their self-image. The description of Australia as 'the biggest Sergeants Mess in the world' was a pretty apt one. The New Zealanders were of an entirely different disposition. Quiet, self-effacing and more English than the English, they were easier to deal with, more predictable but perhaps less fun than their Aussie counterparts.

But we all spoke the same language... or did we? They say that most people learn bad language and smut before general vocabulary and prose when they study foreign languages. Indeed, we all know that in English there is now one word, used as just about every article of speech, which might even substitute for a language itself. Given this, it is surprising that we (the English) had no knowledge of the Aussie verb 'to root', which has a similar earthy meaning.

Peals of laughter rang out when one of my English team announced that the bevy of Australian nursing sisters would be 'rooted' this way and that to their final destination. Nobody picked up on it and the giggles, even from the Kiwis, continued for weeks as passengers were 'routed' in all directions. It was left to Fennings, my surly Australian Cargo Officer, to spill the beans, as it were. I dread to think what innuendo lurks in that phrase. He was, to my mind, 'bolshie' at the best of times and my need to formally inspect his cargo shed was beyond his comprehension.

Notwithstanding his reservations, the inspection went quite well until I noticed a forklift truck askew against a back wall. I had sweated blood to acquire the minimum of mechanical handling aids in this former outpost of empire and the sight of one apparently abandoned and cast aside irritated me more than I can say.

"What's the problem with that machine?" I asked, with an edge to my voice which left him in little doubt that I was singularly unimpressed.

"It's rooted," he said, implying that this explained everything.

"What do you mean, *rooted?*" I went on. "Do you mean that it's not getting an electric charge?"

"Nah," he exclaimed (I hesitate to say 'ejaculated'). "It's rooted ... yer know ... *rooted* ... f**ked."

All suddenly became clear.

34. Down Under

At least our involvement with the antipodeans all but guaranteed a visit to Australia and this was to be before the work at Tengah really started. Every year the Queen invited GC and VC holders to England. The whole exercise required an aircraft to do a round tour of the Far East, collecting them all up and returning them three weeks later. This being the case, the aircraft was empty going out to collect and empty coming back after the delivery. There was massive competition for the places but five seats for the Holland family were guaranteed. The first stop in Australia was a place called Townsville, in Queensland. Logic told me this was a good place to aim for.

The VC10 headed off over Sumatra and the lush islands of the South China Sea and when Australia appeared I thought we were almost home. However, it seemed like an eternity, flying over endless stretches of desert and bush, before we learned that Townsville was in sight. The airfield, like much of Townsville would prove to be, seemed temporary, with corrugated metal roofs much in evidence. A sort of mining town where, sooner or later, when the gold ran out, the population would move on to find new areas to exploit. Only two families got off at Townsville, us, Jim and his wife Margaret, Australian friends stationed at Tengah. Jim would later feature in my flirtation with boats but for the time being they were useful contacts to have in an alien world.

The Movements Officer I guessed was called 'Bull Amos'. My deduction was entirely based on the fact he introduced himself as being 'Bull' and the fact that as we waited for transport in his office I noticed the word Amos was written on his office ruler. I thought it a strange name but it was only after calling him Bull a number of times that my son, little Peter, asked me why I was being so formal. I pointed to the ruler. Peter suggested that the word AMOS might mean 'air movements officers'. My excuse was tiredness but Peter had no excuse for being a 'smartarse'! Bull Amos – I never did learn his Christian name, arranged accommodation in a down town hotel where we were soon all tucked up and asleep.

The next morning we were called by telephone and asked what we wanted for breakfast 'but...'

"But what?" I said. Ignoring my question the voice then offered a variety of foods including steak and eggs and once again finished with the word 'but'. This time I grasped the concept that 'but' was a figure of speech rather than a conditional something or other. Anyway, after a bit more 'butting' we had our huge steaks and made off for 'Magnetic Island', one of the many islands of the Great Barrier Reef.

Some miles off the coast at Townsville, Magnetic Island is reached by ferry. It is fairly big, about five miles across at its widest point. We were to spend many happy days at 'Alma Den', a hotel complex which stood on beautiful shining sands overlooking a coral lagoon of deep blue sea.

On the beach, whether it was over indulgence in swimming or fear of a shark attack while the big boom ready for that eventuality was slack, I really cannot remember. It may have been an attempt to burrow through to Granny in England. It might even have been an experiment to show that water, filtered through sand close to the sea, would be brackish but drinkable. But whatever it was, the hole was not really a good idea and might easily have collapsed with disastrous consequences. Nevertheless, a hole was dug by the children and me which was to excite comment all over the beach. It must have been six feet deep. However, with no sign of water in the base, I waited till no one was looking and poured some in. No sign of Granny and nobody could be tempted to drink the water at the bottom. Despite this, I felt that a sound lesson or two had been learned by all and more importantly, the children were tired out.

The next day we followed a country trail and saw lots of very large kangaroos bounding about and a 'Black Watch' soldier hiding behind a rock. Back at the hotel, there had been many kangaroos, wallabies and wallaroos – a kind of mixture between the two – but no soldiers, Black Watch or otherwise. The climate was wonderful after the continuous muggy heat of Singapore and the children slept well without mosquito nets. Indeed, it was really quite cold at nights, so much so that once Kerstin and I shared my pyjamas, bought in Singapore and seemingly designed to clothe the limbs of a gigantic Chinaman. We laughed so much that we woke up the man in the room next door.

Before the island had a chance to become claustrophobic, we set off to visit Jim and Margaret in Cairns, via the Atherton Rain Forest. We went to a sugar plantation and a crocodile farm and spent a long time with the koalas, 'roos, bats and snakes. The children loved it and Krissy seemed to have a real affection for animals and quickly won their trust. She was not happy with the feeding arrangements for the crocodiles, which were thrown live, day-old chicks. She managed to save one little furry yellow bundle, which she hid in the bush. Even then I think she knew it was a lost cause but at least it had escaped the jaws of a crocodile.

We stopped at one hotel for refreshment and David and I, away from the others for a while, had a small glass of beer each. I think it was described as a 'snort' but it was delightful and David, aged about eight, was very proud to have shared this initiation with Papa. The beer was 'Cairns' which later, try as I may, I could not pronounce without getting a 'can' of beer – any beer, instead. Before we left this hostelry, I signed the visitors book and was surprised to see that an ex Group Captain of the RAF – Black Mac, 'a man who rode horses' – had visited just a few days earlier. Small world.

We stayed with our friends in a well laid-out caravan park with swimming pool *et al* and looked around Cairns, a provincial city that looked a good bit more permanent than anything else we had seen. Jim and I visited a Retired Serviceman's Legion (RSL) club and were served canned beer rather than 'Cairns' draught beer, all because of my English accent, or so said the elderly barmaid, who insisted she too was British despite having lived almost her entire adult life in Australia. This aside, I was struck by the loyalty to the crown displayed by the whole company. At nine thirty on the dot they all stood and sang 'God Save the Queen'.

Green Island is just off the coast of Cairns, an outcrop on the Great Barrier Reef and a great tourist attraction. You could get down to the reef itself via glass tunnels or sit in a glass-bottomed boat and view the depths below. We did both and revelled in the spectacle of glorious creatures of every size and shape as they darted, hovered or glided over the intricate coral – a marvellous spectacle of colour and light. However, from the rather pessimistic commentaries at the time, you could have been forgiven for believing that all the fish would soon be eliminated by swallowing beer can rings and that the coral would be destroyed by the dreaded Crown of Thorns Starfish.

We happily made our way back to Magnetic Island to enjoy once again the delightful fresh fish, less beer rings, which we had for breakfast every morning and savour our last few hours in that lovely place. Why was it ever called Magnetic Island? Well the story goes that a less than competent, possibly even intoxicated, helmsman on Captain Cook's ship drifted way off course and convinced Cook that the island off their bow was magnetic and had interfered with the compass. It seems the island was then so named and recorded and nobody was prepared to admit to the mistake because, whatever it is, it ain't magnetic.

The aircraft glided in gently as the sun went down, actually and metaphorically, on our antipodean adventure. With the help of one of Bull's colleagues, the aircraft steps went in and we were aboard and airborne in a trice. The commanding officer of the squadron, a Wing Commander, was flying the VC10. As I joined the crew on the flight deck I overheard him ask the navigator why on earth they needed to have stopped at Townsville for a couple of 'indulgees' (freeloaders).

No doubt I could have come up with a smart answer but was content in the knowledge that he did not know I was one of that breed and that, had he thought about it earlier, we might have been stranded thousands of miles and pounds from Singapore.

35. An Identity Crisis

You would have thought that having so many brothers and sisters I would have sorted out any identity problems by the time I got to be in my thirties. However, because Paul was known by the resident Royal Artillery Regiment and Peter was such a precocious child, I became known as either "Paul's brother" or "Peter's dad", especially the latter.

For example, when the Bishop to the Armed Forces visited the island, he spent some time in the local school and took a shine to Peter, who seemed to know everything about his vestments and ecclesiastical accoutrements. He also answered all his questions accordingly. Hardly surprising then, having invested so much time in cultivating this rapport, the Bishop concluded his visit by saying that he felt sure he would see Peter at Church the following Sunday.

"No you won't," says Peter.

"Why not?" says the Bish'.

"Cos I'm a Catholic, aren't I."

On the day he left, the Bishop was so keen to tell me all about Peter that when all the other passengers were loaded and I was about to invite him to get into my VIP car to go the two hundred-odd yards to the aircraft, now heating up despite the air conditioning units banging in cold air, disaster struck. Our resident padre intervened with an invitation to the Bish' to 'make use of the usual offices'. Unclear as to what was meant by 'the usual offices' I hesitated long enough for the bishop to escape through the lounge to the general toilet area.

I waited what seemed like an age, at least long enough to receive a message from the aircraft's captain asking where his VIP was. I angrily told the Padre to go and get him and a few moments later followed him to the 'bogs'. I arrived in time to see the hapless priest jumping up and down outside each cubicle in turn (and there were many) saying, "My Lord? My Lord?" whilst onlookers stared, no doubt assuming that the poor man had lost his faith and was seeking it in unlikely places.

"My Lord, the aircraft is going," he finally said loudly and at that the Bish' emerged, dragging up his trousers and pulling his braces over his shirt whilst holding on to coat and accoutrements. Even then, his last words to me were to ask me to remember him to Peter!

One day I was accosted by Warrant Officer Wiggins, who apart from being in Catering, a service we relied on for 'in flight meals', was also a struggling golfer. Wiggins had come out with us on the same flight from the UK, so was already familiar with the family.

"That little sod of yours..." he greeted me with on this particular morning. "Yesterday," he went on, "I had just 'topped' the ball when Peter strode past, club in hand almost as big as him."

"Never mind Mr Wiggins," says Peter. "I've done that myself."

"I almost wrapped my club round his head," says Wiggins.

Only one of my officers, another Peter, was a bachelor, much pursued by single and married ladies alike. He was a likeable fellow and was both the victim and perpetrator of practical jokes. As a victim he was often caught out by Jim, our squadron warrant officer, a diminutive Lancastrian with a wicked sense of humour, who liked nothing better than taking messages from Peter's lady friends and admirers and misreporting them to extract maximum embarrassment.

I was vaguely amused by all this, unless it impacted on the squadron or me. At least twice it did. It was the day of the visit of Her Majesty the Queen. I had sent Peter up country to do a task in Malaysia and, just a few minutes before the Queen was about to arrive, we got a call over a dreadful line. The message was 'Tell the Kiwis not to sing'. The New Zealanders in question were two smart young chaps in tailored white overalls, whose task was to push the steps into position for the royal aircraft and then stand at attention at the side of steps until the Queen and her entourage had disembarked.

Warrant Officer Jim was despatched post haste to the aircraft pan as the aircraft turned onto the approach, to learn that for several weeks Peter had been rehearsing these unlikely lads to sing the national anthem. No doubt the Queen would have been amused, if not astonished, had that telephone message not been received.

"Don't do it," he said. They didn't.

Peter's only practical joke on me, played even after I had given him valuable advice on how to resist the advances of a certain lady who should have known better, was during the 'round the island race'. This was a race – proceeds to the Red Cross – around every hotel and watering hole, finishing at the Singapore Hilton, where the cheque was to be handed over in the presence of a Government Minister. Much could be written about this, including the fact that, given expenses, the cheque came to so little that the amount was never actually mentioned. Furthermore, to the great embarrassment of all concerned, the *Straits Times* newspaper, in reporting the event, chose a photograph of two Singaporean officers from a nearby radar unit, dressed as Catamites, in full female attire, one sitting on the other.

Peter was as anxious to get me involved as I was *not* to be, but when he suggested I should be a judge, I felt a little flattered and foolishly accepted. Means of transport around the island was up to the teams concerned. One team chose bicycles and this was the one I was chosen to judge, not, as I had thought, from the top floor restaurant of the Hilton hotel, sinking cold drinks, but following the team on the oldest, heaviest and slowest bicycle known to man. In and out of traffic, dodging rickshaws, street traders, other cyclists and the unwashed masses of downtown Singapore, I was probably the last person to arrive at the Hilton, hot, flushed and determined that the young rascal would swing for the misery he had inflicted on me.

But I'm too kind and besides, I am 'Peter Holland's father' and 'Paul Holland's brother'.

36. Penang and Babi Tengah

I used to have long 'operator assisted' calls over the jungle telephone with 'Sqidileder Ernie Botherer' in Butterworth, an Australian airfield on the island of Penang. Our first encounter had been by
signal messages, when he had been the boss at Richmond, a big
transport base in Australia. He was constantly sending aircraft
through Singapore to Butterworth, which required us to offload the
entire aircraft to get at the stuff for Singapore. He was subsequently
posted to Butterworth and I was cordially invited to meet him as he
transited through Paya Lebar, the civil airport. A huge man, with
hands like hams, Ernie Booth briefly acknowledged me before
asking where the hell this rude bastard Peter Holland could be
found so he could twist his head off and stuff it down the dunny.
My head remained pretty well intact and after this Ernie and I got
on rather well.

It was with Ernie's help that we first visited Penang. The capital is
Georgetown and aside from golden sandy beaches, some memorable views over the sea towards Thailand and a few sleeping Bud-
dhas, my only real recollection of the place was the funicular
railway. Kristina solemnly made the sign of the cross before step-
ping aboard, much to the amusement of the rest of the passengers.
Poor Kristina had been in some pain from her ears since the Australian crew of the Dakota, which took us from Singapore to Penang, had entrusted David and Peter to fly the aircraft. David did a
famous Biggles trick and the plane dropped a few thousand feet
before recovering. Shortly afterwards, on the decent to the approach, Kristina's ears caused her so much pain that we had to
climb and do a very slow descent.

Because of the capture and internment of my brother by the Japanese, I was sensitive to the history of the place. It seems that the
threat of Japanese attack was dismissed by the colonial government
and the British. Promises were made of steadfast support for the
Malays but the first and significant bombing attack on Georgetown
saw the rapid disappearance of officials and expatriates. The locals

were abandoned and were not quick to welcome back their former masters when the war was over.

Perhaps emboldened by our visits to Penang, we set off on holiday to Mersing, a port on the East Coast of Malaysia. This time we ventured forth by car across the Causeway into Johor Buru and north along jungle roads, where we saw working elephants and a lot besides. From Mersing we embarked on an open motor fishing boat for an island off the coast called Babi Tengah. By the time we boarded it was already late afternoon and, as so often happens, a major storm blew up and ice cold rain pelted down. The children soon gave up looking at the flying fish which leapt all about us and sought what little protection there was.

We came ashore close to an Atap hut. The straw-roofed four-roomed hut stood on a raised platform above the sand and was the only shelter on the island. On the shore to meet us were our friends Don, his wife Adair and their daughters, who were of a similar age to our own children. Don was a navy doctor and his first action was to rush us all up to the hut and give all hands a tot of rum. Sadly, earlier experiences on a frigate off Portland at a tender age had set me against rum, but the rest of the family enjoyed it well enough.

There followed a wonderful week of sarong wearing independence, totally cut off from civilisation. The beach was superb and the sea a blue lagoon, fringed with a coral reef. An abandoned parachute provided endless fun for us all. There were numerous monitor lizards, which sunned themselves on rocks as lizards do, but these were enormous, five-foot-long chaps and rather frightening. Indeed, one chased Krissy off the end of a rocky outcrop. Fortunately, she could swim a mile at the age of five, so easily outpaced the lizard, whose only real interest was to cool off. She was also very good at climbing, but sadly the trees had giant red ants and other itchy things on them, to which she fell prey, propelling herself from the crown of a palm tree into the arms of Kerstin watching anxiously from below. Bugs were everywhere in this tropical paradise, even when we swam, sea lice abounded and joined the jelly fish to try and spoil our fun.

There were no toilet facilities – just the sea. We had tinned food but plenty of booze and water, so we survived quite well! Kerstin and I were amused many years later to see that the Swedish answer to reality television was to abandon contestants on this desert island to suffer twenty-four hour surveillance as they fought for survival. We told the incredulous Swedes that this was the place we took our children to on holiday!

We spent one or maybe two nights in a government rest house in Mersing. Superficially alright, the place was crawling with fleas. If memory serves, we stayed two nights because Kerstin managed to get food poisoning and was unable to travel. I remember standing on the shore and thinking that in 1942, only a few miles off the coast, two capital ships – *Repulse* and *Prince of Wales* – were sunk by Japanese aircraft soon after their fighter cover had to return to Singapore. Thousands of sailors perished and the whole area is a designated War Grave.

Back in Singapore, Kristina now became very ill. We thought it might be malaria but we had taken Paladin and used mosquito nets. In the event, I believe she had sand fly fever. Whilst always alarmed when our children were ill, we were seldom far from medical help and I was often reminded of all those prisoners like George who endured so many years of privation, sickness and suffering. That dreadful war which was a sinister backdrop to my childhood and had ruined the lives of so many, even on the sunniest day haunts us still.

There remains much unsaid about our stay in Singapore: about our *amah*, Ang Mai Lee, called 'Mary' and her interaction with the children; of the children's foibles, especially David and his threats to leave home and go off into the jungle, only to be stopped by the promise of bread pudding; of Peter and his readings in church from behind an enormous podium from which only his little copper top could be seen; of Matavi, my half-Indian and half-Chinese PA; of countless encounters with many nice people and a few bad'uns; of the priests, especially Father Kelly, my Dominican friend. One day I may expand on these memories but for now, enough.

37. The Joke Warfare Establishment

Singapore was a great success for me and I began to believe that a full career in the RAF was possible, provided I did the right things. It seemed that attendance at Staff College was essential if I was ever to become a Wing Commander, that is, if I could expunge the fact that I had taken and failed the Supply Branch promotion examination numerous times before passing it. I thus started up the slippery slope of promotion in the knowledge that my contemporaries could poke the finger of scorn with some justification. Now, having succeeded in the Movements world, I was to have another appointment which was 'out of branch'. I was a generalist and thought it was the specialist, bespectacled nerds who got on.

I became an instructor at the Joint Warfare Establishment on Salisbury Plain. Our chief instructor was a dapper little Royal Marine colonel, who spoke like 'Monty'. He decided to introduce a system of course critiques in which our students were asked to tell us what they thought about us, so that we could sharpen up our instructional techniques.

At the first such open forum he said, "Well, it's over to you chaps now to tell us what you think of us."

A humourless Prussian colonel was the first to react.

"I do not understand why you tell so many, so-called jokes," he said. "You start off every lecture with a joke, mid-way through you pause and our concentration is lost while you tell another joke, and at the end of the lecture you feel obliged to tell us yet one more joke. The Russians are a very formidable enemy. Do you think with these jokes you can make them die laughing? You had better change your name from The Joint Warfare Establishment to The Joke Warfare Establishment."

My sojourn at Old Sarum was a strange one. I learned a great deal about the various military disciplines, doctrines and tactics from psychological operations to air defence. As for my specialisation, the success of every integral part of a military venture rested on Logistics, a subject which the military experts were happy to leave to the 'Loggies'.

I can remember a Brigadier in the Army Air Corps trying to show how he could stop a massive Soviet tank attack by using a small fleet of light helicopters armed with air-to-ground missiles, combined with a force of RAF Chinook helicopters carrying soldiers equipped with anti-tank weapons to be landed in the predicted path of the enemy armour.

The armed helicopters would somehow escape the hail of fire from the enemy by hedgehopping. As an ex-cavalry officer this concept appealed to him – an air cavalry attack – but in my mind I could see something between the 'Grand National' and the 'Charge of the Light Brigade'. He argued that you could pester and harry these tanks into going down a particular route, chosen in peacetime, to where the anti-tank units would be lying in wait. To my amazement, somewhere between herding the tanks and blowing them up, he paused and said, with a certain gravitas, "...and then there is the important subject of Logistics." After a short pause he went on. "Having mentioned Logistics..."

As a committed 'Loggy', I was not spared the withering humour of 'operational types' from any of the three services. Perhaps the rudest and most apt came from an American who wrote: 'Try as I may, I cannot get a cockstand over logistics'.

Military logistic support is both a national and single service responsibility. NATO and UN Commanders must expect forces placed at their disposal to have all the necessary support to enable them to operate effectively but the national resources are jealously guarded and at best can only be co-ordinated by outsiders. Even within nations, for the most part each Service provides its own support to meet its specific requirements. This is because armies, navies and air forces operate differently and match their requirements accordingly. The path of the 'Joint Service' logistician is therefore fraught with difficulties, which are further compounded in an international force. I was to spend some time in this situation. However, in the short term, these anomalies helped me to spend time with the Navy because, as far as I could tell, they had no uniformed logisticians at all.

The most exciting task was to find a way to provide fuel for Navy helicopters to operate in Norway after their carrier had left for re-tasking in an anti-submarine role and before they could access the Northern European Pipeline system. After some alarming trials using a landing craft with a huge pillow tank aboard, in which the most significant failing was that the boat tended to capsize, we started using big rubber containers which could be towed by a Land Rover when ashore and fitted side by side in the landing craft. This did not capsize and allowed the boat to be used for other things.

All this required my presence at sea aboard HMS *Intrepid*, a big command ship carrying a marine commando unit and nine landing craft in its dock, each capable of carrying thirty men or ten fuel containers. I was also required to go ashore with the marines and the fuel containers to prove the concept. Landings were made at Lulworth Cove, where a lifetime ago I had gone ashore as a young sea cadet for our march back to HMS *Osprey* in Portland, the place of my birth.

The JWE was invited to lecture to the Norwegian and Danish staff colleges in Oslo. We were flown in a Norwegian Hercules C130 and allowed to take our wives. Socially it was a great success. Kerstin managed to infuriate the Brigadier by telling him on one occasion when it seemed we might be unable to ski that, had she known, 'we' would not have come; so managing to make herself sound regal or me insubordinate.

But I get ahead of myself.

It was a very cold day when we left Lyneham and a friend, a US Marine Corps Lieutenant Colonel, introduced me to 'Southern Comfort', which we drank from disposable paper cups. I was con-vinced that this was a woman's drink and, against his advice, drank several cupfuls. My memories of the rugged snow-clad Norwegian coastline and the sound of Grieg playing in my head were to leave a lasting impression on me, enhanced, I'm sure, by being in an alco-holic haze.

The lectures were to take place in Akasus Castle, used by the Ge-stapo during the war and now preserved as a war museum in which the various tortures used by the Nazis were displayed. My subject was 'Logistic Support of Amphibious Operations', most of which was gleaned from US Marine Corps publications, a torture in itself. This was hugely irrelevant to NATO, who could never envisage the need for an opposed landing. What a pity we did not have the experience of the Falklands War to call upon. To make matters worse, the team expected the course to break up into syndicates and complete an exercise we set them. At Old Sarum this involved a late evening finish, with teams still arguing with each other in the bar until late at night, but in Norway, at 4pm on the dot, everyone went home!

However, most importantly we got to ski. Suffice to say my efforts were appalling and earned me a prize from the trolls for making the most holes in their snow. The prizegiving took place at the Norwegian Air Force Officers Club in Oslo, following a delightful evening, during which my marine friend and his wife entertained us, singing folk songs and accompanying themselves on guitar. We were all amused to discover that in the song 'Old Macdonald's Farm' all the animals made different noises in the different countries represented. For example pigs in Scandinavia say 'nuff-nuff', in America say 'oink-oink', whilst in England they make a rather snotty, snorey noise.

38. An Old Flame or a Flicker?

Perhaps it's a woman thing which enabled Kerstin to claim, without fear of contradiction, that an 'old flame' of mine now lived three doors away from the Army accommodation we had been allocated. She had taken Kristina and David to their new school in the local village. The only memorable things about that school were the wobbly teeth, loosely connected to the wobbly mouth of the Headmaster. Conversation for or with him was an endurance test; the teeth threatened to scatter at every syllable he uttered and the listener, with eyes riveted on the contest going on in the man's mouth, could rarely remember anything he said.

However, it was not the Headmaster who Kerstin chatted to that day but an Army officer. He was bringing his daughters to school and one was in the same class as Krissy. A nice enough chap, he quickly saw the advantage of sharing the 'school run' chore.

"I'll talk it over with Fee," he said. "I'm sure she will agree."

That was it! She was called Fee, so in Kerstin's mind she must be my old fiancée, whose old engagement ring she still wore with just a touch of resentment.

Fee and I had met years before. She was the daughter of a senior officer and despite strong opposition from her parents on religious grounds – shorthand for 'Catholics have big families and their wives become drudges' – we became engaged. In fairness, the views of her parents were somewhat reinforced when they discovered that I was the thirteenth child! We enjoyed a good social life. Apart from the Mess we had lots of friends and attempted most things, from Scottish country dancing to 'am-dram'. We used to go to night school in Grimsby and when she was finally accepted for a university place, most of my weekends were spent in London, where we found a new circle of friends.

Her absence during the week in London left me at a complete loose end. Other friends emerged to fill the vacuum and I suspected that the parties we went to in London didn't stop for her when I left on a Sunday to face the long drive back. I think the crunch came when her university results were poor and her parents were convinced that this was my doing. It all coincided with my being accepted again for flying training. At twenty-five, on a short service commission, I am sure her parents thought that there was too much uncertainty about my future to entrust their only child to my care.

At this juncture her father was posted to Germany and she went with him. In fairness, she didn't really have much choice. Once in Germany her letters to me became more and more 'matter of fact' and less and less frequent. Of course, for me, our communications were a lifeline from the effort and anxiety of ground school. So when I needed her most she was not very supportive and when I was suspended from flying training she chose to disengage altogether.

Despite or perhaps because of my forlorn letters, I heard nothing from her until I arrived at RAF Chigwell, a radio repair unit in Essex. A cold communiqué from her told me that her father was visiting London and would post our engagement ring back to me. So that was that. The flame had finally flickered out. Or had it? A visit home to see my mother, who in my absence had moved from our comfortable little house into a top floor flat in Hastings (great for her heart!), would present a sea change in my life – it was by the coast.

Despite my mother's warning of the perils of dancing on the pier, I met Kerstin. Within two weeks, and using the now redundant ring, we were 'engined'. By the time she left to return home to Sweden I knew that she was always going to be part of my life. A visit to Sweden and an exchange of gold rings was a further commitment. I was very happy with Kerstin but by the end of my stay I began to think I was swapping one potential mother-in-law who thought me unsuitable for another with a similar view. But this is not about parents, except to say how they can influence their children's choice of partner and how I hope that we might escape that charge.

Back in Chigwell, I learned that Fee had been phoning me in my absence and later that same day we spoke. There then followed a week of madness in which I was, to quote the old song, 'bewitched, bothered and bewildered'. I wanted to escape from the whole dreadful dilemma but held back, remembering the feeling of trust and contentment that Kerstin had given me. Fee went back to Germany but wrote to me for a few weeks. Then, nothing.

"Here she comes," Kerstin called out to me. I stood back from the curtained windows, feeling like a 'Peeping Tom' and convinced that it would not be her. But it was! When we called on her a few days later there was no hint of surprise and in subsequent meetings during the few months we stayed in Army married quarters, our previous friendship was just not mentioned.

During the intervening years Fee's mother had died and her father, who I had always admired, had remarried. He visited one day and we chatted for some time about the old days. I was glad that I was now a squadron leader and could boast an MBE, which he also had.

"This is a rum business," he said. "What a turn up for the book." He was right, and this is the book! Our encounter made no difference. Fee would always have a special place in my heart, as first loves do, but we had both clearly chosen wisely and it provided a good yarn about probability and coincidence. It could never happen again, could it?

39. Those Who Can't, Teach

Of course I kept trying to get onto one of the staff college courses, considered essential if I was to make any further progress, but it seemed an unlikely outcome. Another route was to press for a further Movements job at Brize Norton, which could just land me the Senior Air Movements post – a Wing Commander – but I should have known that first they promote people, then they find them posts! My wish was granted and I got my command but it was of the Air Movements School – an independent command and a Squadron Leader post! Worse than this, I had never done the Movements course myself, yet now I was supposed to deliver it!

Suddenly, all this was as nothing, driven from my mind by the death of my mother. She had been unwell for some time and towards the end she chose to live with my brother Alby and his wife Margaret. They looked after her very well and my niece Joan, who was a nurse, used to visit regularly. One night when we were in Hastings with Kristina, more by chance than anything, I went out for the evening with family. Kerstin stayed behind and talked at length with my mother. In the early hours of the following day, with Joan in attendance, she died peacefully in her sleep. She was much loved and dearly missed by children, grandchildren and great grandchildren.

Some years before she had written out a will, leaving my house and the cooker to me! Various items of furniture, oddments and linen were to go to others. Amused, I pointed out, as kindly as I could, that my house was not hers to leave and I doubted anyone else would want a second-hand cooker. With that, she discarded but did not destroy the document, which was neither signed nor dated. Unfortunately, in the intervening years she disposed of most, if not all, of her things, even the front room clock; often pressing them on people who didn't want them and seldom, I suspect, to the people she had originally chosen as recipients. It was therefore embarrassing and uncomfortable when the unsigned will was discovered amongst her belongings and worse still when folks called to collect. A cautionary tale but it is just the sort of thing that happens amidst the awfulness of death – so look out anyone who thinks they are getting my ivory chess set! Be kind and tolerant to me in my dotage and we will play chess in heaven.

Peter and David had by now left us to go to Boarding School. For Peter, who was already at Bishop Wordsworth's Grammar School in Salisbury, this would be his ninth school. David joined him on the same day as his sibling, leaving only Krissy with us. It was a miserable experience leaving the chaps at their school, with its smell of stale something – perhaps sweaty socks. It seems it wasn't much fun for them either; the bullies were out for them. Peter, never changing, always stuck his neck out and David, much more flexible and accommodating, caught at least some of the flack meted out to his brother. But perhaps that's a story only they can tell.

Krissy, having had a short spell in a private school in Salisbury, now moved to the RAF School at Brize Norton. We were very proud to see her doing so well at ballet, once performing for Dame Alicia Markova in the new Salisbury theatre. However, she was painfully shy and apart from the continuity of education we felt it would do her good to board. Had we known the treatment being meted out to our sons we would never have sent her. As it was, it was painful enough to see her go to join her brothers. I had got so used to seeing her at lunchtimes and watching as she waved till she was out of sight. We missed our children more than they could ever have understood and almost resented having to go through the whole painful farewell exercise every exeat.

The RAF Movements School was an independent command lodged at Brize Norton but controlled by the MoD. For the first time, I had my own pennant fluttering atop the RAF ensign. The job was interesting. I spent a long time fighting to get a big establishment increase and there were numerous trips to Malta and joint courses with the Army and Navy. I tried to expand the notion of 'Movements' to cover the whole science of distribution rather than concentrating on movement by air, always the exciting bit. I hoped for and advocated the creation of a separate Transport and Movements branch, but it was not to be.

I like medals, especially if you do not have to dodge bullets or jump through hoops to get them, but the Queen's Silver Jubilee came and went and I didn't get a medal again, having also missed out on the Coronation gong. However, my colleague who ran the Army Movements courses at Aldershot did get one, as did a junior officer on a local squadron, 'honoured' for his diligent management of a social fund and subsequently cashiered! Was it too much to expect that *everyone* who had proudly served the Queen for 25 years should have received the medal? I wonder if anyone asked her.

40. The Pickle Factory

After only nine months at Brize Norton and totally out of the blue, my longed-for promotion to wing commander came through, accompanied by a posting to Brampton in Bedfordshire, Headquarters of Support Command. I was to be the Command Movements Officer – not Air Movements but Surface Movements – that is to say, 'trucks and trains'. I also controlled the RAF's Mobile Explosive Teams and several Movements units in Belfast and London, as well as No.2 Mechanical Transport Squadron at Stafford.

This was a job I loved, in a delightful part of the country, and it proved to be one of the happiest times of my Service life. In the office I was able turn what might have been a pretty humdrum experience into a lot of fun by playing 'Star Trek', then a popular TV show. I gave my various officers the names of characters from the series. My office became the Captain's Quarters and the general office the Operations Room. Suddenly, the game paid off. The Ops Room became the central hub of all the many activities. The introduction of computer systems enabled us to maximise the use of our freight capacity and trace consignments, as well as controlling and communicating with our various units and teams.

I enjoyed a good social life with good friends and colleagues. Then there was Ann-Marie. After thirteen years we suddenly had another little girl. The children were delighted. Kristina became a little mother and the boys almost fought over who should push the pram. Kerstin's pregnancy had been a worrying time for us, made somewhat worse by having a doctor as a neighbour who believed Kerstin had waited too long to have another healthy baby. Even over the table at a Mess night, he warned me to be sure to get an amniocentesis check for Kerstin before it was too late.

Kerstin and I were duly tested. For me it involved no more than a blood test but poor Kerstin had to endure considerable stress whilst they prodded around, trying to extract some amniotic fluid. Finally, after extracting only a little blood, Kerstin gave up for fear that the baby would be damaged. We said a little prayer and went home, prepared to accept what would be.

On a somewhat lighter note, my other next door neighbour was one of those chaps who did everything well. He was a mountaineer, a terrific gardener, a wonderful mechanic and, I gather, a marvellous husband. The last quality I could only take his wife's word for but the rest – well let me give an example or two.

I found him once in his garden, in the snow, crouched over a steaming pot that was perched on a makeshift fire.

"Strewth," says I. "Has your cooker packed up?"

"No," he says. "I'm practising for the Himalayas."

His garden was always perfect and weedless, his cold frame full of tomato plants and with runner beans actually running somewhere. My garden, in contrast, was anything but, with only the odd rusting bicycle growing amidst the bindweed. His garage had shadow boards groaning with bright shiny tools and he had one of those roller boards on which you can slide under cars to see what's what; from the roof hung a hoist to take engines out! Have I said enough?

Anyway, this fellow, a Squadron Leader, invited Kerstin and me to dinner to meet his boss, who was a soldier.

"Do you know Fee and her husband?" says my perfect neighbour, convinced that this social mixing could do nothing but good for his career and blissfully unaware of our previous encounters. After a few amused hums and coughs, I think we all had a fairly relaxed evening. I never bothered to enlighten him.

A senior colleague used to love motorcycles, frequently a topic of conversation during our trips together on staff visits to far-flung units. One awful day, his son died in an accident in which, I understood, his motorbike was stationery. I felt so sorry for him and very reluctant some months later, to lend my much loved 'Vespa' motor scooter, which had served me so well voyaging between Wilton and Old Sarum, to my son Peter. Much to his surprise, in his first week at University, I was hugely relieved, to learn from him that it had been stolen, burnt and written off.

My boss was an Air Commodore who looked for all the world like Ronny Corbett, and not much taller. He knew how to treat people, win their respect and command their loyalty; often rare gifts in those chosen to lead. One day he told me that if I wanted further promotion, I would need to work in main stream 'Supply'.

Of course, I neither expected further promotion nor did I particularly like the idea of doing 'Supply', unless it was an operational job like command of the Tactical Supply Organisation, which supported RAF and Army helicopters in the forward area.

I was therefore surprised when, out of the blue, I was posted to nearby RAF Henlow, which had become the entire world of signals and communications, all in one location, and was now grandly called The Radio and Signals Engineering Establishment. It was commanded by an Air Commodore who rejoiced in the title of Commandant. Apart from his headquarters staff he had a major functional unit consisting of a factory and several other operational elements, called the Radio Engineering unit, whose commander, a Group Captain, was also the station commander.

I was to command the Supply Wing and answer to the Group Captain. This reminded me a bit of the complex command structure in the Far East and I decided from the outset to answer to anyone with rank! Inevitably there would be minor issues between the Air Commodore and the Group Captain, who were entirely different characters. The Group Captain was a large ex pilot-cum-engineer with an ebullient, rude and robust manner, whilst the Air Commodore was a smoother, quieter person, looking rather like the actor David Niven. I had great admiration for both of them.

Henlow airfield itself had an historic identity crisis of its own. One of the oldest airfields in the RAF, it was forever getting mixed up with Hendon, equally antique, which between the wars became internationally famous for its air tattoos, the forerunners of the Farnborough Air Shows. It is said that a certain Air Marshal, convinced that more hangar space was necessary at Hendon, approved their construction but, in the telling, confused the airfields. When he was told, far too late in the process to do anything about it, he is reputed to have said "Oh what a pickle!" The hangars in question soon became known as the Pickle Factory and were put to a variety of uses over the years after the main function of the unit became the RAF Engineering College, in which generations of officers were trained as engineers.

Shortly after the Second World War, one of the Commandants of the College commissioned a young artist called David Shepherd to record, on a set of table mats, pictures of the many aircraft which had flown from Henlow in its early days. The task was undertaken at seven shillings and sixpence each. History does not record exactly how many there were or how often they were used, but on a wet day shortly after I arrived, one of the cooks, doing an apparently long overdue clean-out of old cupboards at the back of the Mess, stumbled across about a dozen of them. He had the good sense to ask his Flight Sergeant whether he should throw them away. Under the grime the NCO saw and recognised the signature of the well-known artist and saved them from the bin.

The pictures were cleaned and displayed in a single frame and hung in the anteroom. One of my first duties as the President of the Mess Committee was to welcome David and his wife to a ladies guest night. During the evening he told me how he came to do the paintings for a pittance and how, soon afterwards, he left for Africa in search of more old wartime aircraft. If I recall correctly, it seems that in an Officers Mess in Kenya, he talked to an ageing pilot who suggested that as he was in Africa, he would do better painting elephants! He took the advice and soon copies of his elephant paintings bedecked the walls of the masses and he went on to do wonderful things. He was a kind, modest man and Mrs Shepherd was delightful. It was a memorable occasion.

The Pickle Factory had at one time been used to test and develop parachutes. Apparently scaled-down models were used and the parachutist was a small dog owned by the corporal in charge of the tests. The dog would be released from the rafters and float gently down to the ground and no doubt was in receipt of parachute pay by way of a treat. The experiments continued for quite some time, with no harm done to the dog, until one day, not far from the base, the dog and his master were both killed while the dog was riding pillion on the Corporal's bike, sadly before the days of the ejector seat. Legend has it that sometimes at night you can hear the little dog yapping.

The Pickle Factory was used in my time as an overflow for the RAF Museum at Hendon and contained in many ways more interesting things than those on display at the museum. I was forever seeing things which had been so familiar when I first joined the service but were now totally forgotten, from fire bells and buckets to fire engines, ambulances and staff cars, all mixed up with the technical detritus of flying machines.

My first interview with the Group Captain was really very revealing. It seems he had overwhelming professional admiration for my predecessor, my remit, therefore, was not to touch too much but to go and put a smile on people's faces. I was also to be PMC and deputy station commander. This was the home of engineering and he must have known he was taking a chance. Shortly afterwards he took his first leave and I was left in charge, maybe the first supply officer ever to command this Engineering Unit.

We lived in a lovely old house originally the station commander's residence, it nestled in a corner of the camp, surrounded on three sides by open farmland. There were other bigger residences, inhabited by the Commandant, the station commander and various wing commanders. Technically my house was now not big enough to warrant domestic help but the others were. The Group Captain intervened. As I had four children, one of them a baby, we were to have some help. The mess manager allocated us one of his team.

Now she was a pleasant, hard-working and respectful lady who bore a striking resemblance to a well-known northern comedian in drag although nobody, least of all me, would ever mention it. Nonetheless she was a good soul. She used to hoover and dust around son David when he was at home and in bed and she was forever picking up little Ann-Marie's toys and her 'sot sheets' (rag comforters). She simply became part of the family.

The Station squash courts were close by the house and Peter and David, who I had first introduced to squash at Old Sarum and who now played at County standard, were quick to prove that I was well past it. Krissy too could only be beaten when I feigned exhaustion and held my heart.

The Commandant was a thoughtful and charming man. He seemed to like the Holland tribe and was touched when Krissy called him Uncle Niven and baked him a cake. He also accepted Kerstin's direct speaking and understood that I tried my best to walk a careful path between him and the station commander in matters to do with the Officer's Mess.

The Group Captain was an excellent public speaker and expert in poking fun and delivering withering criticism. The ruder and blunter he was, the more people enjoyed the speech. Our American friends from nearby Chicksands Priory, which he referred to as 'The Slough of Despond' (this was Bunyan country) thought he was an absolute riot and his own officers considered themselves badly done by if, when they were dined out, they were not soundly berated. Fact was, he actually meant what he said!

The Falklands war crept up on us at Henlow, where most of the radar, secure speech and other communications equipment was manufactured, repaired, calibrated or modified before being distributed worldwide. Everyone worked extremely hard and tactical communications units were deployed. For some reason I thought I might be called on to head up a special Tactical Supply unit which would go out on the QE2 but this was highly unlikely because I was not technically qualified – not that that had ever stopped them before. As it turned out, a former colleague from Singapore was to lead the unit and when I discussed it later with him he modestly downplayed his part in what was, no doubt, a complex joint-service structure in which his unit certainly did valuable work.

Everyone was very gung-ho about the war and part of me longed for action but, if I am honest, this time I was relieved not to have to put my head above the parapet. I kept remembering the young man who died in my arms so many years ago and wondered privately whether, in the long run, it would all prove to be worth it. Not a popular point of view at the time.

Mind you, we had some 'make-believe wars', for this was the era of the TACEVAL or tactical evacuation. In this exercise a unit is suddenly and without warning visited by a number of directing staff who tell you that war has been declared. In the next few hours, with the operations room manned, the unit goes through the war books as each measure is called until finally you are on a war footing. For an engineering unit this involves making and repairing vital equipment, preparing people and equipment for despatch to the airheads and ports of embarkation, taking precautionary security measures, manning ground defence positions and protecting essential facilities.

We had no RAF Regiment officer at Henlow but I had been one, so the ground defence plan was put to me to draw up and complete. I will spare you the detail but one of the principles of defence is to include in the defensive layout vital installations. Terry Scott, a well-known comedian of the time, or rather his double, was our 'works and bricks man'. He owed his allegiance to the Department of the Environment and believed he owned everything and we were borrowing it from him.

Relations between the Station Commander and 'Terry' were strained from the outset for both were determined to exercise their authority to the full, with disastrous consequences. I had planned to have armed guards behind a wall of sandbags outside the main guardroom at the gate to the camp. It was rather an elaborate guardroom, built at the beginning of the century, with columns supporting a grand façade at the front. The station commander decided that the guards should be on top of this balcony, com-manding a better view of their surroundings than they would at ground level. That was OK, the balcony would well support two or three men on it, but the construction of a sandbag emplacement to protect them was clearly out of the question.

The Group Captain, anxious to impress the TACEVAL team, was not prepared to accept this. The first row of sandbags was laid before word got to 'Terry' that his buildings were being got at. He fumed, he snorted but the sandbag wall continued to grow. He cajoled, produced plans and diagrams but the bags grew and grew. At last the job was done ... and the whole front of the guardroom collapsed.

The Boss next turned his attention to the station water supply, which was served by a pumping station that was well outside the Station bounds and an enclave in a farmer's field. This must be secured to prevent disruption or contamination by biological agents. When he arrived at the gates he discovered they were pad-locked. Undaunted, he had the padlocks cut, strode in and posted the sentries.

Back in the operations room, 'Terry' confronted the CO.

"You'll get Weil's Disease you will... and so will the sentries," he warned. "You and they should visit a doctor as soon as possible." The ground defence commander – me – having never heard of 'Wheels disease' and thinking it an affliction of the bosses, fell out and wiped his sword.

Apart from being 'Defence Commander', Deputy CO and President of the Mess Committee (PMC), I was also the senior catholic officer on the base. We had no resident priest when I arrived and priests were hard to come by, but not long into my tour they found one, late of central Africa. I will call him 'Father Brown'.

41. Fall Out the Roman Catholics and Jews

"Father forgive me for I have sinned, it is a week since my last confession and I have been impure with my sister!" There was a stir from behind the curtain as, I suspect, *The Racing Times* fell onto the knee of the Parish Priest as he waited to hear more of the activities of this debauched seven-year-old.

"Yes my son, can you tell me a little more about the story?"

Surprised, I replied, "Yes, it was the one about an Englishman, an Irishman, a Scotsman and a pound note... but she had heard it anyway."

I never told my sister. After all, confessions are secret.

Cautious doubts on matters religious crept in at a very early age, cautious because the very soul is threatened by doubt. Perhaps the first issue of substance on which I made a stand was 'Peter the Hermit'. He inspired the ill-fated Children's Crusade to the Holy Land, a subject touched on during Religious Education. It is unlikely that Father Lynch admired the antics of this particular 13th Century cleric but he was clearly taken aback by my scathing remarks about 'that lunatic'.

It was not long after this outburst that the college Rector, over dinner with my father, was full of praise for my brother Paul, who shone in everything he did.

"As for Peter," he said. "I think he might be an atheist."

This, no doubt, was chickens coming home to roost for 'our George William', as my aunts called him. The son of a lay preacher of the Wesleyan persuasion, he had been received into the church 'under a gun carriage' in the First World War – or so he had us believe. Although his knowledge of the Bible was encyclopaedic, I suspect that his faith ebbed and flowed with the sound of gunfire or the threat of death.

His Sunday chore was getting us all off for church and preparing a feast for our return.

"What did the priest have to say this morning then?" was a standard question, as the eggs, tomatoes, bacon and fried bread were being washed down by tea. Whatever the answer, he would demolish it. If it was church dogma, it was dismissed out of hand as claptrap. If it was scripture, it had been misquoted or taken out of context. Hardly surprising then that Peter was an atheist!

Both Rector and my father were wrong about me, however. Indeed, I even thought about becoming a priest but my kind of God laughed a lot and took our part.

"Dominic go frisk 'em" instead of *Dominus Vobiscum* would have given Him a giggle too. The Jesuit way did not square with this at all. Perhaps it was the *ferula*, a thick strop made from whalebone covered in rubber, which made me think again about a commitment to a regime which could inflict so much pain in the name of God. Had things moved on all that far from the Inquisition and the Conquistadors?

It was at this moment in my young life that I was to leave Yorkshire and the 'Js' behind for a Grammar School in Hastings, founded by William Parker in the reign of Good Queen Bess. Suddenly there were no morning masses or afternoon benedictions, no decades of the rosary, no divine praises, just a hymn after assembly, but to my surprise, I and a Jewish friend called Alan Stein were always excused. I made up for it during lessons, however, when the opportunity to argue with the bearded and much-married divinity teacher proved irresistible. Despite this, I began to feel that I no longer quite belonged.

"Fall out the Roman Catholics and Jews!" rang out across the Parade Ground. No mistaking this dilemma. It was a case of 'stay and deny your faith' or 'go and demonstrate your un- Britishness'. I went, but from the edge of the square I heard the Padre recite The Lord's Prayer. What nonsense not to stand with my comrades and say the prayer that Christ himself had given us. Next time I stayed. Much later I learned that to leave was a concession to my faith and not an exclusion from that of others.

I visited war-torn Jerusalem and stood on the Mount of Olives overlooking the city, certain of my faith at one moment and sure the next that I was sustaining an ancient myth. My father, oh yes, he returned to the church he had vilified so much. After his confession he told me that the priest didn't mind a bit. I'm not at all sure what he meant, but confessions are secret.

Confessions were never secret, however, with Father Brown. Deaf as a post, he used to say, "Speak up, I can't hear you." So it was possible that the whole congregation and half the camp knew of the indiscretions and misdemeanours of the penitent suppliants.

"Oi don't know why the sacrament of reconciliation is less popular here than in moi last parish," he would say. But his last Parish was in darkest Africa, whence, it was unkindly rumoured, he may have been moved on for overindulgence in the 'hard stuff', but certainly not through lack of piety or faith. Whatever the story, we were blessed that Father Brown was appointed to minister to our spiritual needs in our little chapel at Henlow. However, he found it necessary to consult me daily, if not hourly, about his personal administration and he was naïve in worldly matters. Indeed, he became a constant source of irritation.

"Do up your seat-belt Father."

"To be sure it's broke but when I see the police fellahs, I'll pull it over me."

At last, in answer to my prayer "will no one rid me of this troublesome priest" he was taken off my hands by, of all people, the non-conformist chaplain, who taught him all the means by which he could get his allowances and entitlements, how to behave in the Mess and no doubt fix a seat belt or deal with the police.

For all that, he was kindness itself and he *believed*. At our last service in that chapel he bade us farewell and, to applause and cheers, presented the family with a crystal vase bought by popular subscription and a little book in which was written 'Lord I believe, forgive my unbelief'.

Now I try to look for Christ in everyone I meet, although He is sometimes very difficult to see! But, as I look back, He was there in Father Brown.

42. Hit Me Again, I Can Still Hear Him

The story goes that, after a long and monotonous speech, the President at a service dinner tried to hit the table with the gavel to announce the end of dinner. In his anxiety to be away, he didn't notice that the Station Commander's head had slumped forward and now intervened between table and gavel, whereupon the 'old man' looked up with vacant eyes and said, "Hit me again, I can still hear him."

Now I have no way of knowing the truth of that story but I can sympathise with the spirit of it, since the dreaded Plodger left. It had been a good evening up to that point in the old Officers' Mess at Henlow. I was to be the next President of the Mess Committee, so was taking mental notes on the proceedings and enjoying myself in the certain knowledge that, for the foreseeable future, I would not.

Plodger rose to speak.

"I joined the Service in 1949," he began. I was immediately reminded of the pilot who told his best friend that he had not had sex since nineteen forty nine.

"Crikey, that's a long time ago!" his friend said.

"Not really," said the pilot. "It is only twenty hundred hours now." My thoughts were brought back with a bump when I heard Plodger describing, at some length, the young men who had joined with him. Surely he was not going to detail every event in his Service life, or was he? Please God let it be a spoof. Any time now he was going to tell us that it was all a leg-pull. We would all laugh and drink his health.

But God was not listening, or if He was, it was to Plodger.

No man was too unimportant to get a mention in the chronic chronicle. Around the room there was the occasional good-natured "Hear, hear" up to the 15 minute point, but this gave way to stunned disbelief and then sullen resignation as the quarters sounded off in everyone's mental clock.

It might have been the shellfish that did it, or perhaps the mixture of peppermint chocolate and other delights on top of my brandy. The reason did not seem important. The fact was, I felt sick. It started with a wave of nausea fairly easily suppressed as I tried to concentrate on the shiny nature of Plodger's drill instructor's accoutrements – a funny word that. It got a lot worse. Plodger was still 20 years from finishing when the waves became more frequent and bordered on the retch.

I looked frantically for an escape route. Did the heavy curtain behind my chair conceal an open window? If so, could I make it into the garden without throwing up? I even had sympathetic thoughts for Plodger, which he did not deserve; what a terrible amen to his farewell speech to hear me 'honking' in the background. The antidote was water. Of course! Drink lots of water. So I did. A whole jug. The sickness remained just as acute but by the time Plodger was within a decade of home my mind was taken off the impulse to be sick by a dire need to relieve myself.

"...and so, my friends, it only remains for me to say thank you all and to ask my fellow guests to drink your health." Gasps of relief and mutterings of "thank God" echoed around the room, although there was little to thank Him for. Clearly even His level of boredom had been broached. For me, I was at my wits end. The gavel hit the table, I got ready to dash away, when, could I be hearing right? The President was agreeing to a request that Plodger should drink the health of the Royal Air Force. This seemed to necessitate him starting all over again!

By now, the sweat was pouring down my face. Death must be better than this. Then, in the way that cataclysmic events so often finish, it was done. I stood up, downed my port, opened the curtains and dived through the window. Delicacy forbids me to dwell on the details of what followed but the occasion was imprinted on the grass for weeks to come and on my brain forever. Armed with experience of that evening, I have been circumspect about what I eat and drink at official functions as well as ruthless (when able to influence such things) about the length of after-dinner speeches.

I might have done well to have considered my own efforts in that direction more carefully.

"My Lord Bishop, Air Marshal Davies," doing well so far, "Distinguished Guests, Commandant, Station Commander," soon be there, "Ladies and Gentlemen, Air Commodore..." Suddenly my mind is a blank. Our principal guest looks at me in anticipation, ready and waiting to leap to his feet and get his own agony over. There is no relief, no door through which to escape, no friendly prompt, no way in which I can now rephrase the invitation to speak. There is an uncomfortable cough, the agony continues... Suddenly I have it. "Davison!" The word is shouted as desperation gives way to relief. The effect is pure music hall.

Could it happen again? Only once! Several years later, in even more sumptuous surroundings and in distinguished company, I was to welcome the Deputy Commander in Chief to the mess and call on him to welcome our new Commander. Once again, the litany of names followed by, "Air Marshal, Sir Kenneth..." This time the sense of *déjà vu* was added to the blind panic that ensued. I remembered that the name was associated with the body. Name association has never been successful in my long experience of introducing Mr Partridge as Mr Bird or Wing Commander Pope as Wing Commander Monk and always haunted by the story of the young officer who introduced his ladyfriend Miss Fluck as Miss Clunt. The body: Leg? Foot? Head? Yes, there was a ring about that, something about the head...

I had heard only that week a distinguished raconteur and distant relative of Edvard Grieg (not that this had any bearing on his abilities or on my predicament) talk about public speaking. As a doctor, he said, he was amazed by the durability and versatility of the human brain that began to work almost as soon as the cluster of cells making up the human body began to form. It continued to operate unremittingly day and night through infancy, childhood, to manhood and only ceased to function when the poor man whose body it inhabited was called upon to make an after dinner speech.

That must be it! Brain! It would have to do. Time had run out. "Brain", I whispered, applying at least one lesson from my earlier experience.

With a withering glower, Air Marshal Sir Kenneth Hare stood up to speak.

At Henlow the family were growing up quickly. Peter was accepted for a place in Canterbury University, which gave him the opportunity to use Hastings at weekends when he wasn't commuting back to Hitchin and thence to Wales to play soldiers with the SAS. David was to follow him to a degree course at Wolverhampton whilst Krissy remained at Boarding School. The joy in our lives was Ann-Marie, who was such a clever little girl, whose only major failings were an aversion to owls, a hatred of cars and a propensity to lie down on the floor and scream in shops.

In so far as we had an owl in the tree outside her window and Kerstin's pastime was shopping, this made for some sleepless nights and some very sicky car journeys, rewarded by lay-down protests when we finally reached our destination. But Ann-Marie was nobody's fool. This was evidenced one day when we were visited by one of my two squadron leaders, a very serious, tall fellow with a fine old English name which did not flow lightly over the tongue, whom I had unkindly nicknamed Fazackerpan, by which name he was soon universally known.

Ann-Marie was on her 'trike' in our lovely rose garden when he called on us.

"Hello little girl," he said, slightly stooping and looking down his nose.

"Hello Fazakerpan," says AM. A young lady of few words.

43. Us Bloody Europeans

My two-year tour at Henlow flashed by and I was posted to the 2nd Allied Tactical Air Force in Germany. 2ATAF, as it was known, was a NATO force which had a skeleton staff brought up to full strength in exercises and war by all the NATO air forces in northern Europe. In war the headquarters would move to underground caves in Maastricht and the commander of RAF forces in Germany would take charge.

I was Chief of Materials and Movements and answered to the Assistant Chief of Staff Logistics, a Belgian Colonel. Funny thing about Belgians serving in NATO, depending on how they feel, their working week begins or ends on Wednesdays. So for the most part I was ACOS Logs. My fellow Lieutenant Colonels all arrived days after me, which in NATO made me the senior. They all accepted this except one, who, because he was actually more senior to me by time in rank and was Chief of Policy, felt aggrieved that this English upstart was boss.

Everyone on the staff spoke German, including the Frenchman and my American Captain. Everyone, that is, but me. If I had been posted to RAF Germany, the national headquarters, I would have completed a language course. However, as both English and French were the official languages in NATO, if you spoke either of those you couldn't do the course. As it happens, this caused me no problems because all the others, except the Americans, also spoke good English and when I finally took my leave of them all, I gave my speech in French. But it was my English rather than my logistics skills which was most called on, translating American English into something comprehensible to other Europeans.

The first part of our stay in Germany was at a small village called, or at least pronounced, Waldniel. It was some several miles from the large base, almost a garrison town, called Rheindahlen. We stayed in a very large flat, used all the local German shops and were very happy. In my last week at Henlow I had been given an RAF bicycle, with a pennant affixed to acknowledge my role as Deputy

Station Commander. The award was made in the Sergeants Mess –
a rare honour.

The bicycle, less pennant, was now used by Kristina to explore
the countryside and by me for her marathon training. She used to
run saying, "Why? Why? Why?" as she breathed out whilst, from
the relative comfort of my steed, I would reply, much to her irritation, "Because, because, because."

Kristina was now a beautiful young woman who turned heads
wherever she went. She was a terrific artist and woodworker, very
athletic and enormously strong. Whenever she was with us, she was
a great help with Ann-Marie, not the least when Ann-Marie was
unwell.

Ann-Marie was not very healthy during our stay in Germany. At
first she would not eat and we were becoming desperate until
Kristina came to the rescue, giving her twiglets, cocktail snacks and
Nutella, making a game of it until, after much encouragement, she
started eating again. But there was more ill-health to come, especially when we moved into a house at Rheindahlen. Apparently, on
the advice of his fortune teller, this was the only German garrison
not visited by Adolf Hitler, because it was unhealthy. Not that Ann-
Marie had anything in common with Adolf.

Peter had, in the dying days of our stay in Henlow, without my
knowledge and still playing soldiers, applied for the RAF. He passed
his degree course and was accepted for pilot training within a few
days of each other. At the time we were convinced he was setting
out to kill himself one way or another. Anyway, we now attended
his graduation ceremony at Cranwell and travelled back to Rheindahlen by air. We left the following day by car for Oberammergau
in the South, the land of mad Count Ludwig, home of the Passion
Play and a NATO Training College. We paused in Rheindahlen only
to clean out our very large freezer, which the errant child of a kindly
disposed neighbour had turned off when Mum was checking the
house. It was to be the first time I was able to put my service respi-
rator to good use!

Our journey south was remarkably uneventful. Ann-Marie managed not to be sick until we were a mile from the hotel. Despite the
travel sickness, we had a lovely time in the village and enjoyed

swimming in the heated pool, part under cover but mostly out in the cold air and snow. There was no Passion Play whilst we were there and snowdrifts prevented Kerstin and Ann-Marie from reaching Count Ludwig's castle. I had a jolly time learning more about the business of extermination and we were able to do a little skiing, even Ann-Marie, on her little red skis.

I also got some clues as to the Carnival and Oktoberfest celebrations. I had been appointed PMC of the NATO Mess. A bit odd really because we shared the Mess with RAF Germany, who had a Group Captain PMC, and we always felt like a poor relation. It was my task to organise the Oktoberfest and I had already learned from my Prussian General that only Catholics and Southern Germans bothered with such things. So there was massive disinterest on all sides but everyone expected it to be done right for all that, and so it was. But I run ahead of myself...

Soon we were heading back to Rheindahlen and Ann-Marie seemed fine. This time we dared to hope that she was growing out of the travel sickness problems. But a few days later she had tonsillitis. She stopped eating again and was obviously unwell. Following two visits to the RAF doctor she was rushed into hospital with suspected meningitis and although after a lumbar puncture, a dreadful procedure, she was shown not to have this, she did have a collapsed lung and double pneumonia. It was a terrible time having to leave the poor little lass in hospital. Kerstin and I were beside ourselves with worry. Every morning at our daily briefing my colleagues would ask after her as the first item on the agenda. All were relieved when she turned the corner.

We bought windsurfing boards and sails and Kristina, Kerstin and I learned to use them in a rather nice area on the German Dutch border called Roermond. There was no doubt who was the ace, Kristina of course. Kerstin and I did our best but, oh, it was so difficult and at forty nine (!) thought that I was past such things. I tried subsequently to use the boards in Hastings when we came home but found it even more difficult. For her part, Kerstin was able to get on the board but unable to steer it. On one occasion she started off in Hastings and I had to drive along the coast road to rescue her near Bexhill! Needless to say, Kristina did the actual rescue.

My visits to the caves at Maastricht, just over the border in Holland, were most memorable, especially during the long annual exercise called 'Wintex'. The caves were very extensive and had been used by the Dutch resistance during the war. It seems the Germans were never able to sweep and clear them. Another part of the caves had, in medieval times, been used as a monastery and apparently many monks had been buried down there. In its new role, entrances and exits had been largely sealed off and at the front there was a huge steel door. The whole reminiscent of a James Bond film set.

There were hooters and alarms for all manner of things, a public address system rather like that of a ship and an inadequate ventilation system which reminded me of being submerged in a submarine. This was not helped by a general mess canteen from which the smell of coleslaw oozed to the furthest enclaves. Our logistics enclave was made particularly objectionable by the cigar smoke of our German Engineer Chief, from whom I almost always took over.

I spent my fiftieth birthday underground, listening to "Exercise, exercise," followed by this alert or that, in case we got confused with the real thing, longing for the one when the Warsaw Pact countries revolted and the Russians caved in. It always happened just before total annihilation was ordered. At last I could have a shower, get back to normal and enjoy a late birthday.

Back in the office, I heard rumours that someone in the Supply Branch was to be promoted to Group Captain. I supposed it would be an officer on the staff of RAF Germany and went off to consult with such a man, of whom I thought quite highly. He seemed perplexed and uncomfortable. Maybe he already knew that, against the odds, the new Group Captain to fill probably the most important Supply post in the RAF at Strike Command, was me.

ACOS Logs once more, it might have been a Tuesday. I received a note from the Office of the Commander in Chief asking ACOS Logs to pen some words that the C-in-C might use to say farewell to a certain Wing Commander Holland at a forthcoming Guest Night. I chose my words carefully, using such words as consummate skill, dedication, personal and professional integrity, a leader of men. I finished with the words 'us bloody Europeans will miss him'. I signed it off, 'Acting ACOS Logs'.

At the Guest Night the C-in-C read it out in its entirety, pausing only to say that the Acting ACOS was me.

Before I left I met up briefly with Fee – Yes, you've guessed it, her husband was on the staff of the headquarters. She wished me well and I never saw her again, although some years later, again by chance, I sat beside her husband on one of several aircraft going up to a training area in Scotland.

But as twilight looms, who knows, we might one day make a foursome at Bridge!

44. Cincafuk

Headquarters Strike Command now combined all the operational commands, that is Bomber, Fighter, Coastal and Transport Commands, as well as most overseas elements. It seems that when it also took on a NATO role, the 'Natospeak' for its new name was to be Air Forces UK. The Commander was to be known as C-in-C AFUK. Direction signs had already been erected all over Oxfordshire which said simply CinCAFUK. This was pronounced 'sinkafuk'. Apparently, the Commander did not like this name and despite protests from NATO, never sensitive to our Anglo Saxon ways, the headquarters was renamed C-in-C UK AIR – Not a FUK in sight!

Strike Command was to be my last proper job in the RAF, combining prestige and opportunity in what was, for me, a unique and rewarding experience. How I got to be appointed was always something of a mystery. The job specification called for a staff college graduate. I wasn't. A qualified fuels expert. I wasn't. A graduate of the Air Movements School. Well, I wasn't that either, although I had commanded it, apparently under false pretences. He was also to be a top flight supply officer. I think my several attempts to pass the promotion exam gave the lie to all that.

Perhaps it was, after all, down to achievement? No doubt all this had a part to play but the real reason I was appointed was because my new boss, an Air Commodore, never an easy man to please, had already rejected out of hand several highly qualified officers who had been proposed. In frustration the personnel people had dipped their hand into a bucket of names of people yet to appear before a promotions board and came up with mine. This caused a furore amongst my peers, of whom at least two found themselves working for me! It didn't please my boss either. He was ambitious and demanded highly qualified support. He didn't think I was it.

Things came to a head when he decided to have a heads of branch meeting with the wing commanders and me. Also invited was his dog, 'Major'. After an interminable period of time and when I was getting particularly restless as he droned on about widgets,

Major snored. A barely audible little snore at first – I managed to stifle a giggle – but gradually the volume grew and I looked round the room at the others. Not a hint of emotion. I looked up at the ceiling but the snore followed me. I had to get a grip. I had almost made it too, when suddenly the dog farted! This unexpected development sent me over the top. I stood up and said in the deepest, sternest voice I could muster. "Excuse me Sir, Gentlemen, I need to speak urgently to my PA." With this I rushed out.

The Air Commodore came into my office, sat down and, in his dark velvet voice, said 'You don't fool me. You were laughing at my dog weren't you? You're a giggler. Well I am too and I like you. You're very much like me, perhaps that's the problem.' I doubt that anyone else would have agreed with this sentiment but he then recounted to me the real story behind my appointment and pledged that he would do his best to get on with me. I felt damned by faint praise but was touched after he left, when one of my most senior wing commanders came to give me advice on how to handle the old man.

It was almost two years before the promotions board caught up with me, but I had the rank and the pay, so what!

One of the first things I did was to return to Germany to prepare a joint presentation on a plan to disperse aircraft from their main bases to operate from remote locations unlikely to be the target of enemy action. The Swedes had been doing it for years and it had been the basis of my own thinking and actions for some time. Anyway, my visit enabled me to call in on my old division where my Dutch colleague was now the deputy. He had been less than enthusiastic when I had been promoted, so after I had listened to his dream plan for his future, I casually mentioned that I was to be promoted yet again – a lie but it was worth it.

I was very lucky with my colleagues at the headquarters, I had a good team and perhaps because of my Regiment and Movements background the operational staffs regarded me as one of them and called me 'bombs and bullets'. I was able to stress the importance of logistic support to all their plans and the limitations that time, distance and quantity can impose. They listened and allowed our plans for the co-ordination of this support to be a vital component of the war-fighting role of the Headquarters. I was very proud, on my last day in office, to be down in the huge underground head-quarters in the Logistics Centre, which I had largely planned and set up, to be thanked by the Commander in Chief and his predecessor, who was now the Chief of Air Staff. We were only months away from the Gulf War, in which the system would be proved.

TACEVALs such as we endured at Henlow hit headquarters as well but most important was the annual NATO-wide exercise 'Wintex'. One particular day, in the middle of this fortnight-long exercise, we were visited by the Prime Minister, Margaret Thatcher, who was to be briefed by the 'Battle Staff'. I was the Logistician. I must confess that I felt a degree of trepidation, knowing that sooner or later I would have to give my logistics brief and not wishing to misuse that opportunity. However, hardly had the intelligence brief started before she gave her own take on the situation, based on her visits to NATO headquarters all over Europe. I need not have worried. Like most people, she never got down to Logistics!

The discussions continued elsewhere with the C-in-C until we reached the usual bit in the 'Wintex' scenario, when the Warsaw Pact countries mutinied and 'The Wall came down'. Now I have no means of determining the veracity of the story, but it was said that the C-in-C expressed the view that it might happen anyway and that Mrs Thatcher told him this was naïve; if true, an opinion most people at the time would have shared. However, not six months later I was acting for my Air Commodore and sat at my desk watching the daily briefing from the headquarters staff. Dramatically, we were beamed over to Germany to watch the extraordinary scenes as the Berlin Wall was torn down. Finally, that dreadful war which started in 1939 and had pervaded and shaped our lives, was finished.

If I am honest, I enjoyed the dignity of rank and the social life of the Mess, so, when towards the end of my service I was asked to become PMC of this the premier mess in the Royal Air Force, I could not refuse. Clearly this was going to be a tougher job than Henlow, although there were some similarities. The Mess was under the direct control of the C-in-C. The unit commander, a wing commander, had no influence over it except physical command of the men working there. The job involved much hosting and presiding. My dinner companions were almost always the C-in-C or his deputy and the guests were invariably senior commanders or politicians.

Overall I did alright, although I did have some problems with the 'flower ladies', as I had at Henlow, determined as they were to make every 'Dinner Night' a festival of flowers. Furthermore, the activities of the Ladies Club, known as the 'Thursday Club', caused me some grief. I decided to warn the C-in-C in a speech about their diverse and sinister activities, telling him that any idea he might have that the power lay amongst the 'colonels' was misguided, whereas if he were to cross the Thursday Club, he might find himself hanging by frangipani under Blackfriars Bridge. I was jesting but my new boss was not amused – his wife was the chair of the Thursday Club!

45. Santa Lucia

'Damn, Damn, Damn. Bloody road. Silly woman!' Why was I going to an alien church and why were we late? The great doors of the old Swedish Church in London were closing when we arrived, the service started, the congregation squeaky-clean, necks strained, eyes disapproving as we clattered our way to a space towards the front. I tried hard to understand the Pastor. A word here, a word there, the sermon droned on. What was I doing here? Then a hymn. Goodness, I knew this one. OK, so my Swedish was awful, but who would notice?

There was a shuffle at the back and children's voices singing "Santa Lucia." I felt a twinge of emotion as they made their way up the aisle. I stole a glance at Kerstin. Some would have seen a middle-aged woman, her cheeks drenched with tears. I saw a beautiful girl, her eyes gleaming, clutching a bouquet of flowers, herself pondering why the hard-bitten old official was dabbing his eye so many years ago in that dingy Registry office. Had our marriage made up for all that she forswore that day?

The general's wife was Swedish and thrilled to meet a compatriot at a recent Mess function. A kindly, bubbly lady, indeed a titled lady, she demanded to know where and how we had met.

"At sea," I said, hoping to elicit a cheap laugh from the fact that we had met on Hastings Pier.

"So did we," she said, not allowing me to elaborate further. "Well, not exactly at sea. It was on my father's yacht in the Suez canal." Her 'husband to be' was an Aide to the Governor of somewhere. I had a vision of opulence that dwarfed anything I had experienced and the rest of my story remained untold.

More memories came flooding back. Our first born son, such a beautiful child, no one like 'lille Peter Lars'. Indeed, to 'Sus' (Kerstin, as pronounced in Sweden, was a name too difficult for an English ear), no one like his papa. Then there was David, then Kristina and, when we thought we were just too old, Ann-Marie. There was Cyprus and babies, Singapore and Sumatras, Australia and coral reefs, Norway and snow, Rome and ruins, Canada, the States but for her, seldom home... "Santa Lucia".

The previous year we had enjoyed 'Baby' Peter's wedding and soon we would be grandparents. I was proud of the pomp and glitter of the military wedding; Peter an Officer in my Regiment. Proud too of my family and the opportunity to show them off to my own ageing brothers and sisters. Kerstin also enjoyed the moment, but there was no Mormor, no Morfar. Her father was ill, neither travelled abroad and it was not their sort of thing anyway... "Santa Lucia".

This summer's holiday had taken us across Europe to the East Coast of Sweden, soaking up sun and scenery. Fleeting visits to parents and relatives, lengthy discussions about the viability of a Swedish cottage. Perhaps because their view of Sweden is as prosaic as our own, we knew that our children would love the idea. But eventually we were overwhelmed by the sheer impracticability of it all... "Santa Lucia".

Poor Kerstin. Will she ever get her little *stuga* that I long to share with her? Will she one day see 'Lucia' or Midsummer in Sweden? Will we bathe, as nature made us, in the lakes and visit the high mountains? Will we ski and build snow houses and watch the seasons change? Or is it all, like the smell of ginger biscuits, just out of reach?

If Sweden is where the heart is, then perhaps Sweden is in the heart. All I know for sure is that when I squeezed her hand to comfort her, quite unable to speak, her eyes said, *'Jag älskar dig'* (I love you) and I knew that she had a place there for all of us too. "Santa Lucia".

46. Sailing By

I watch Ann-Marie with a mixture of pride and apprehension as she sails off for the first time at the Welsh Harp Youth Sailing Centre. The same feelings I have felt at different times with all the children, particularly around water. I have to confess that our family experiences on the deep have not been universally happy ones.

They started with our Heron, which we bought and sold for a song in Singapore long before Ann Marie was born. The Heron is big enough for an adult and a small person but no one could convince the 'half-Swedish family Holland', that it was too small for us as we launched our new acquisition into the South China Sea – Peter, David, Kristina, Kerstin and me! We knew naught of centreboards or rudders; we could get the sails up, what more was needed?

The 'Rhyme of the Ancient Mariner' was never a favourite of mine but as we drifted at the whim of breeze and tide on the flat, oily sea, I wondered if we would finish up like he, the children, Kerstin and me. The shore was much further away now and it was impossible to pick out the tiny yacht club from the verdant line of rich jungle vegetation. An element of alarm began to creep into the boat as the realisation that we were helpless and lost dawned on us all. The 'Hail Marys' seemed like a good idea but tended to heighten the feeling of impending doom that settled on us all.

"Look a sail! Should we wave for assistance?" The idea was no sooner mooted than done. David broke off his 'aves' to remove his shirt without taking off his lifejacket, in a contortion which defied belief. Within seconds he was waving it and soon help was on its way. After that we decided it might be wise to take lessons! But, valuable though the instruction was, it was hardly up to the elements.

It was not unusual for it to rain in Singapore in the afternoon and thunderstorms were commonplace. It was great sport to be in the warm sea with ice cold rain pelting down, some even sported umbrellas! But, for the intrepid sailor, it was altogether a different matter. The clouds would suddenly bellow up into great grey anvil heads which fill the sky from top to bottom all around, setting a black backdrop against the deep green of the jungle horizon or the slate blue sea. An eerie silence would fall; there would be no wind, sails slack, 'in irons'.

We are all familiar with that little breeze that comes before the rain which tells us which quarter the storm is coming from. Not in Singapore! Lightening connects sea with sky with a blinding, breath-taking sizzle. You smell it on the air, it adds to the tingle of fear, the feeling of anticipation. It starts to rain, big drops of ice cold water then, without warning, the Sumatra hits you. The sails flap, crack and fill, you fight to spill air before you are overturned, the rain bites your face and freezes you to the bone. For the perpetual beginner like me, the fight is on to cheat the storm and survive. For the expert, to get the most out of boat and wind, to grasp an advantage, to win the race, but for all, the transition from sultry heat to bitter cold, beggars description.

When Peter and David sailed off on their Piccolo sailboards and Kerstin and Kristina went together in our little boat, there was no sign of bad weather. Just as well because the safety boat was far away at Seletar Island, with most of the sailing dinghies and their crews, including me and Jim Paine, of whom more later. The wind which sprung up gave them good sport far out in the sea but as it gradually grew stronger it was Kerstin who made her way to shore. David was well in and Peter was following her, she thought. When the full force of the Sumatra hit them, Kerstin was swiftly approaching the shore and Kristina was bravely offering her the life-jacket which David had immortalised.

The sail was down and the boat was beached ... but where was Peter? He was certainly not in the gloom beyond the stony fore-shore, nor 'just behind her'. She made her way to the club house, which stood on piles above the murky water. No comfort or assistance there.

"You," she said to two young men. "Come and help me save my son."

The admiral's barge was moored alongside.

"That will do, can you fix it?"

The two men climbed aboard and, after a little tampering, were rewarded by the throaty sound of a powerful marine engine as it spluttered into life.

Kerstin took up her position in the bow, holding a boathook across her chest and giving directions to the crew as they steered their commandeered boat.

"She looked like Britannia, or was it Rheinhilda? All that was missing was the Elgar, or was it the Wagner?"

The cheeky dialogue used in the telling and retelling of the story has never concealed the relief Peter felt when he saw his mother coming to the rescue on the bow of a naval launch. Blue with the cold and clutching onto a huge buoy off the Jarong Dockyard, he and his adult companion, who he had been teaching to sail, were in serious trouble when help arrived.

The admiral was delighted when I told him the use to which his boat had been put.

"The soldiers," for that is what they turned out to be, "must be thanked" I told their CO. "They showed commendable initiative and you should know."

There was an amused pause at the other end of the phone.

"Perhaps you should know that today I was able to tell them that one had been mentioned in dispatches and the other awarded the Military Medal."

"For saving Peter?" I quipped.

"No," he replied. "For services on special duties."

Kerstin always chose her men well!

"We have plenty of tucker and beer so we'll be right, but we don't have a 'Buckley's' of winning the race, or even being placed."

In this colourful language Jim Payne had assessed our chances that afternoon as we prepared our boat in the bright sunshine but as we drove through the silence of Kranji cemetery at midnight, the rows of white tombstones flanking the War Memorial provided a sinister backdrop against which dreadful watery thoughts were difficult to suppress. The tension was heightened by the far off rumbling of thunder and incessant scratching of crickets and croaking of the frogs; dreadful portents of what lay ahead.

It was uncannily quiet and the river flat and oily as we slid our boat through the reeds of a mango swamp into Kranji creek, close to the causeway joining Singapore to Johor Baharu, shortly after midnight. We were not alone in this adventure, there were dinghies and keel yachts of all shapes and sizes moving up to the start line of this, the longest inshore race in the world. With hearts pounding we were about to begin the 'Around the Island Race' with the finish 18 hours away.

Jim was to be the crew because the ink on his 'sea helm certificate' was slightly wetter than mine. We felt we were a good team. After all, we had sailed solo to the next club, on Seletar Island and put away a quantity of Tiger beer (Singapore's Best) before returning on the tail of the same storm which had so nearly reduced the family. As we planed along on that sunny day, our ambition knew no bounds but in the eerie prelude to the race, both sober and sombre, we agreed that survival would be our prize.

The boats, anchored against a swift-running tide, held their position with difficulty. Lights flickered amongst the motley of vessels. We only had a hand-held torch to indicate our position. The big keel boats had lights; port, starboard, fore and aft. Many were covered in fairy lights and the noise of tinkling glass shattered any illusion that for the crews of these the race was to be anything other than a party.

The whole armada drifted past the start line at the appropriate moment and continued to drift in the fast running tide. There was little that crews could do to control their vessels and the danger of collision became a hazard for the first time. Collision with a boat of comparable size is bad enough but a run-in with a big keel boat could be disastrous.

The Sumatra hit us in the narrow confines as river became sea. We had the means to steer if we could remain upright but the keel boats previously lumbering alongside us were now criss-crossing our path at frightening speed, capable of cutting us in two. Neither were we sure that their beer swilling crews, secure and under cover, were not beyond caring. It seemed our best course of action was to keep close inshore. This would both reduce the danger of collision and the distance we would need to swim if we capsized or were hit.

Keeping close inshore is rather like flying close to the ground, it gives a false sense of security. Always better to have height or sea room. It was not long before this tenet was to be proved. Jim was in the bow, his eyes strained on the spume filled sea in front whilst all around was inky blackness, eased momentarily by flashes of lightning which flooded our own boat with light and froze the outline of nearby boats and shore.

"Ready to go about?" said Jim, his Australian drawl disguising the anxiety in his voice.

"Not yet," I said. "I want to get a bit more speed so we can turn better." I could see the shore through the blinding rain, punctuated by the lightning; it was near but not dangerously so. Whilst long-since shedding the illusion that all Australians were variants of the unflappable Chips Rafferty, I remember wondering about the note of panic in my partner's voice.

"Ready about Pete?" he repeated.

This time there could be no doubt; he was worried.

"Fer Chrissake Pete, go abart!"

I went about and as the boom of the Bosun came across and the big sail filled with wind on the other tack, I saw it for the first time. It scraped along the side of the boat and towered above us like the teeth of a giant comb. It was a *kelong*. Built of bamboo and almost always supporting tiny fishing huts, these seemingly flimsy constructions stretch far out to sea and can withstand huge seas and high winds. A moment later and this one would have torn our boat to shreds.

"Thanks Jim!" I shouted at the wind as we headed out to the open sea.

Soon the choppy inland waters gave way to the rollers of the South China Sea and we made fine progress to Singapore Harbour but as the sun came up, the storm gradually blew itself out. Becalmed, we drifted first this way then that. We could still see plenty of the dinghies that had started with us, some close in, others well out to sea, but all standing still and no sign of keel boats. At first it was not unpleasant to bask in the sun and warm up our bodies, chilled to the bone by the storm and to dry our clothes whilst the flying fish provided an escort to nowhere. It gave us a chance to drink our beer and reminisce over the events of the night. We watched a variety of vessels sail by, ranging from oil tankers, which carried us forward in their wake, to junks of different size, colourfully painted and bustling with humanity.

One thing was obvious, they all had power. It was to be oars rather than horsepower which were to be our painful salvation. We took it in turn for what seemed like hours and gradually, at first almost imperceptibly, in that short twilight of the East we made headway to land in Changi Creek. We travelled to the finish line by bus. Many vessels had beached or capsized, the race had been abandoned and history had been made. Only the keel ships with their radios and their engines had had the information and the means to act on it. Driving half asleep down Bukit Timah Road, now even more dangerous than the native users of that highway, I was content, we had won our prize – we had survived.

For such an experienced sailor(!) navigating around a sandpit in Oxfordshire some years later should not have presented any insurmountable difficulty. My sister Wendy had agreed to sail with me and, like all disasters, the seeds were sown very early in the plot. My buoyancy jacket was fine for Wendy but what was I to do in order to meet the strict regulations which required everyone to wear a jacket? 'Borrow one from a fellow sailor,' I hear you say. Not a bit of it; far too easy a solution. I would borrow one from the RAF's Safety Equipment Store.

Aircrew lifejackets are designed to save unconscious airmen from 'the drink'. Should the unfortunate man wake up, he can blow a whistle, light a torch and activate a safety beacon, all of which will bring rescue by air or sea. You may feel that using such gear in a sand pit borders on overkill. You may be right.

Hugh, Wendy's husband, watched with Kerstin from the shore as we launched into the pond. They had little idea of the entertainment they had in store for them. We were soon underway and everything was under control.

"Should we have a problem," I said, "just let everything go and the boat will come into wind. The sails will flap a bit but we will remain upright. In the unlikely event of a capsize," I went on, sounding rather like one of those stomach churning matter-of-fact airline briefings which strike terror in the hearts of even the most experienced traveller, "I will stand on the centreboard whilst you will roll into the boat as she rights herself, then you simply help me aboard, we bale out and on we go as if nothing has happened."

Almost at that moment we were hit by a strong gust of wind which prompted my sister to let go of the foresail. Perhaps if I had let go of the main sheet before we jibed, or waited till afterwards, we may have survived. As it was, the 'unlikely event' occurred very quickly and in a trice we were in the water. I stood up on the centreboard, Wendy pulled up on her side, I was catapulted off the board and sister and brother faced each other over a totally upturned boat.

At that moment Sir Galahad appeared, a bronzed and athletic man sailing single-handed with the competence and confidence to match his appearance. These people always seem to be on the hover to make my embarrassment complete. He positioned his boat alongside, hove to and scooped my sister out of the water with consummate skill and without so much as a word. He then made off at speed across the lake, leaving me to my own endeavours.

'Safety first,' I thought. Pull the plunger on the old lifejacket, which I had secretly always wanted to do. The gas flooded into the empty lungs of the jacket and its collar attachment with such force that it winded me and my body shot up in the water at an angle of 45 degrees, where I now lay like a recumbent Michelin Man, incapable of any movement except backwards but understandably reluctant to activate a full scale air sea rescue operation.

I floated backwards to the bow of the boat and grabbed a line. Kicking with my legs, I managed to get the boat moving, very slowly, towards the shore. It seemed like an age, with my eyes on the upturned bow and with no way of seeing where I was going, before a friendly voice offered help.

When I re-joined the family, Wendy was flushed with excitement and Hugh was heard to remark in his quiet Scots lilt,

"I had no idea what a splendid spectator sport sailing is. Take the old girl for a ducking any time!"

47. They Only Fade Away

'Old soldiers never die,' the old song says, 'they only fade away'. So it was to be with me. I had bought a surplus married quarter at Hendon, not to be confused with the Pickle Factory. I had in mind that I might spend my remaining months undertaking a study in the MOD and so commute. I will not dwell on this because it was a mistake which I lived to regret. In a flash I lost my friends and a lovely residence in exchange for life on the Northern Line, travelling to a broom cupboard in what I dubbed The Ministry of Darkness and Despair.

Ann-Marie left a school in which she was happy and Kerstin lost her social life – all for a dismal place in North West London, soon to be swallowed up by social housing with all its attendant problems. At the end of the study and immediately before retirement I was to undertake the 'Works and Bricks Course', a City and Guilds course for ex-servicemen held at Aldershot. Shortly before joining the course I was contacted by my former boss, by now an Air Vice Marshal and Head of Branch. He was going on the same course. Would I like to join him in the Catering Officers Mess at Aldershot? This seemed like a good deal – the best food in the Army.

However, I found being 'hoddy' for his bricklaying a bit much, so when the opportunity came during the plumbing phase to give him a soaking, I took it. I also accompanied him to RAF Uxbridge, where he was dined out as the former head of the Supply Branch. In contrast, six months earlier at Strike Command, under mess rules which as PMC I was bound to enforce, I had not been formally dined out because I was not leaving the RAF immediately. I therefore missed the opportunity amongst friends and colleagues to say a fond "Adieu" to the Service that I loved and receive their farewells to complete the circle.

On my last day of active service, Kristina, correctly gauging my mood, took me to lunch at the RAF Club. Kerstin and Kristina bought me a pocket watch, the kind I had always wanted to wear with Mess dress. A lovely thought but when would I use it now?

Perhaps the most poignant moment, for which I was quite unprepared, was handing in my identity card. I felt suddenly cast off and alone for the first time since I was seventeen.

I should instead have been looking forward to 'The Time of My Life', with Kerstin at my side, when I would dream in uniform and wake up in pyjamas.

Epilogue

During almost 40 years in the Royal Air Force I served as airman, infantryman, air defender, fire officer and logistician in joint service, commonwealth and NATO assignments throughout the world, commanded numerous units, saw active service and spent all but my last six months in uniform. It started at the height of the Korean War and finished as the Berlin Wall came down and the Soviet Union collapsed (not that I had any influence on either events!).

During my time Great Britain endeavoured peacefully to dispose of a worldwide empire and remain a power to be reckoned with. Politically it was considered essential to become and then remain a nuclear power, whatever the cost. All our training and efforts were directed towards deterrents but all the actual wars we fought and situations we managed were conventional and some might say, conducted on the cheap. We were party to a series of pacts and treaties designed to deter the Soviets and Chinese from world domination and to protect the commercial interests of the West, including oil.

The Royal Air Force, once organised into Commands and Groups in the UK and geographic Commands overseas, continued to contract. In the UK, Fighter, Bomber, Coastal, Transport, Signals and Maintenance Commands were amalgamated or reduced to Group Status within others and Overseas Commands and their functional components were absorbed into the remaining UK Commands until eventually we were left, essentially, with an operational command and a logistic command. In the same period the Air Ministry was absorbed into the Ministry of Defence and numerous MoD functions delegated down to Command and Station level ... and so the process continues to this day.

In the exercise of air power, concepts of operations came and went but the biggest change was the destructive power of the weapons and the ability to conduct operations over great distances using air-to-air refuelling, transport forces, strips of concrete and little else. The need for large garrisons overseas dwindled and disappeared, to be replaced by detachments and roulements with few, if any, permanent staff and even fewer dependents enjoying life overseas. The logistic support of our forces had to match these changes and to seek economies elsewhere, by joint service and international rationalization, civilianisation, outsourcing and contracting, reduced stock levels and the sophisticated use of IT in all our activities. Less tangible but more poignant was the sacrifice of many traditions and privileges, so often the glue of a fighting force.

In the Royal Air Force the business of flying aircraft is always and properly at the forefront, but the work of ground crews, engineers, suppliers, administrators, caterers and the Royal Air Force Regiment is vital and mostly unsung. If you say you have been in the RAF, civilians brought up on a diet of Battle of Britain and Dambusters stories always ask, "Did you fly?" The need for tactical and mobile logistic support and the physical defence of deployed forces means that the answer can now usually be answered proudly and emphatically, "Yes". We might also add, "and because of us, so could our aircrews."

So, as I look back over my shoulder to my life and times in the Service, I hope that my jottings might help show that the Royal Air Force was, and remains, a wide and rich tapestry woven by many, both in the air and on the ground and there are many good and exciting stories still to be told and many careers yet to be enjoyed.

As to my life as a civilian, the next twenty years or so would be taken up with civic and voluntary work, with writing, painting walls badly and canvasses worse and all the affairs of our children and grandchildren; James, Matthew, William and Peta, as well as our extended family and friends in Sweden, where we bought the family *stuga*.[3] In Hastings, we acquired a delightful detached Victorian house with a tower and ornamental garden.

The story of the Swedish Family Holland continues. In January 2012, Kerstin and I celebrated our Golden Wedding Anniversary by renewing our wedding vows at High Mass in the Ulrika Eleonora

---

[3] Cottage.

Kyrka, the Swedish Church in London. The service was conducted by Bishop Caroline Krook, the former Bishop of Stockholm and the Rector, The Very Reverend Michael Persson.

So, dear family, I may record all this in a further 'work' just for you. 'Hit me again, I can still hear him,' comes an echo from the past.

~ Fin ~